IT'S YOUR LIFE

YOUR ADVENTURE

YOUR CHOICE

IT'S YOUR LIFE

YOUR ADVENTURE

YOUR CHOICE

Don't Just Take What Each Day Brings.

Bring Something to Each Day.

TANYA BLACK

AUSTRALIAN EDITION

COPYRIGHT NOTICE

Copyright © Tanya Black 2009

Ownership of Copyright

The copyright in this publication and its contacts (including without limitation the text, artwork, photographs, images, is owned by Tanya Black in accordance with the Copyright Amendment (Moral Rights) Act 2000.

Copyright license

Tanya Black grants to you a worldwide non-exclusive royalty-free revocable license to: print pages from this publication for your own personal and non-commercial use. All rights are reserved. You must not adapt, edit, change, transform, publish, republish, distribute, redistribute, broadcast, rebroadcast or show in public this publication or any material within the publication either part or in whole (in any form or media) without written consent from the author. Small quotations may be reproduced with citation and reference.

Permissions

You may request permission to use the copyright materials by writing to Tanya@tanyablack.com

Enforcement of Copyright

If you have used copyright materials in contravention of the license above, Tanya Black may bring legal proceedings against you seeking monetary damages and an injunction to stop you using those materials. You could also be ordered to pay legal costs.

First Printed in Australia May 2009.
Published by Bardon Whiting
AUSTRALIAN POD EDITION

Copies of this book can be purchased from www.tanyablack.com

ISBN: 978-0-646-51412-3

Dedication

Inspiration is a Four Letter Word:

A N N E

To the most incredible mother on earth:

I want to be just like you when I grow up.

If I can be to my own children what you are to me, I will know I have succeeded.

I love you.

About the Author

Tanya Black has owned several businesses including an independent Real Estate Agency, a Web design business and a Café. She has used her experience to help others as freelance Business and Marketing Consulant.

When she discovered the many uses of business and marketing systems in personal development, she shifted her focus to helping others achieve balance and direction in their own lives.

Tanya continues to advance her knowledge base and has written this book as a guide to personal transformation and presented the concepts in an entertaining and easy-to-follow format.

She has been painting professionally for 11 years and has entered the Archibald Prize three times. Her art has given her some valuable life experiences. Some of her past sitters are: David Helfgott (on whom the film 'Shine' was based) and Jamie Dunn (also known for his alter-ego Agro).

Tanya lives in the Magic Jellybean Clubhouse on the Gold Coast Australia with her two young sons Dominic and Elijah and regularly posts to the blog on her web site at www.tanyablack.com.

To contact Tanya, e-mail her at: tanya@tanyablack.com

Table of Contents

PREFACE i

INTRODUCTION iii

WHO FORGOT THE TENT PEGS? WHAT YOU'LL NEED vii

PART ONE

PARAMETERS FOR CHANGE 1

Chapter One

Transmutation Class - Overview of Part One 5

Chapter Two

Mirror, Mirror on the Wall - Acceptance 15

Chapter Three

It's all in your Head - Mindset 21

Chapter Four

The Teddy Bear's Picnic - Environment 29

Chapter Five

WT R U TRI N 2 SY - Communication 37

Chapter Six

It was a Dark and Stormy Night - Fear 47

Chapter Seven

How Strong is your Resolve? - Commitment and Discipline 55

Chapter Eight

Goody, Goody Gum Drops - Reward 63

CONTENTS

PART TWO

UNDERSTANDING THE 'WHO' AND 'WHY' OF YOU 69

Chapter Nine

Pulling Apart a Gadget to see how it Works - Overview of Part Two 73

Chapter Ten

Don't Listen to what the Salesgirl tells you. Orange is not you Colour and she works on Commission - Social Conditioning.. 79

Chapter Eleven

Confessions of a Podium Dancer with a Whistle and a Thimble of Dutch Courage - Ego 91

Chapter Twelve

The Dog ate my Homework - Excuses.. 99

Chapter Thirteen

Make the Minutes Count - Time Management 107

Chapter Fourteen

Oh My - What Pretty Gold Teeth you Have! - Financial Management................... 119

Chapter Fifteen

The Love Boat - Love and Relationships 135

Chapter Sixteen

Betting on the Horse with the Coolest Name - Managing Life Changing Experiences.. 147

PART THREE

TOOLS FOR CHANGE... 157

Chapter Seventeen

The Road Beyond the One I Left Behind - Overview of Part Three 161

Chapter Eighteen

Atlantis isn't Lost - We Are! - Mind Mapping 169

Chapter Nineteen

You put your Right Leg In - You Put your Right Leg Out -

Simple Business Principles 181

Chapter Twenty

One, Two, Buckle my Shoe - Daily Success Habits 189

Chapter Twenty-One

There's a Hole in my Bucket - Building Pipelines 201

Chapter Twenty-Two

That's a Cool Bike. Can it do Burnouts? -

Tools for stress management 211

Chapter Twenty-Three

Rome wasn't Built in a Day and the Universe Took Seven -

Taking one day at a time 225

Resources and References - *My Bucket List* - Further Reading 229

Preface

I'll throw in my confession and disclaimer upfront to warn those who are easily offended. Throughout the book, you will find some innuendo, sexual references and colourful language.

I also draw on various religious and spiritual concepts of different backgrounds. Read them as a metaphor and story. I use these examples and terminology because they are familiar to most people and the power of a metaphor lies in the familiar association of one concept to illustrate another.

When reviewing the book, I considered changing the language and some concepts to avoid offending my readers, but in doing that, it would have diluted the strength of some of the metaphoric concepts so I have opted to keep the original content.

This book also contains the occasional shameless plug. This doesn't strengthen the content, it's just a merchandising trick to make you buy stuff...

My new life began in late 2008. It was not an easy choice but one that I knew in my heart was the right choice to make.

When I stepped out on my new path, I took some debts that I intend to honour and a steadfast belief that I can achieve anything I desire. When I turned the page and started this chapter of my life, I set myself some challenges:

> *'By the end of 2009, I will be debt free and I will achieve this doing only that which I enjoy doing.'*

I have been focusing on listening to my intuition, staying positive and being grateful for the wonderful things in my life. This has helped me to stay focused and appreciate the potential I have.

My very own adventure was unfolding. The gifts that I have in this life are a natural love of writing, painting and drawing.

I have always been a storyteller and enjoyed doing these things. Over time, I have developed these skills.

I don't know where my words or paintings come from. Sometimes the message and vision is clear. Sometime it starts misty, but once I get to that place where I lose time, words write themselves and the paintbrush guides itself.

Some messages are clearer and form stronger statements than others. One of these messages has become my personal mantra:

'Don't just take what each day brings.
Bring something to each day.'

It came to me when I was cleaning the garage. I stopped cleaning and wrote it down. I have this statement hanging in various places around my house.

Every day I live by this mantra. 'What can I bring to this day that will take me closer to my ideal life?' It has become a habit and a large part of who I am.

As many of us do, I had conformed to everybody else's ideals of what I should be doing, and I had tried fitting into Society's vision of what a girl like me should be.

I have had the marriage, the picket fence, and the 'stuff' that comes with social conformity and a mortgage.

One day I realised I had lost my smile. It was then I decided it was time I started on a new adventure.

Thank you for taking this journey with me. I hope that I can help you on your own journey.

The first step is to make a firm decision to take the actions necessary to change your reality. Once you have made that first step, just set yourself a goal to take one-step a day. Soon you will find yourself taking two, then three and when the past is a distant shore on the horizon, you will have forgotten how hard it was to take that first step.

Remember where you came from and appreciate how far you have come, but don't hold onto the past so tightly that you can't embrace the present and every opportunity it has to offer. Don't be blind to the riches that are yours now for the taking.

Introduction

"I chose the road of the least trodden path. I walk it every day and it takes me closer to Eldorado. At night when the sun falls on the horizon, the glint of gold reflected in the sky renews my enthusiasm for the riches that await me."

Tanya Black

I have written this book for the reader who wants to change their world but doesn't know where to start.

This book is in three parts.

Part One: *covers the parameters for change. Knowing the theory and techniques offers no value if the groundwork and foundations are still made of quicksand.*

Part Two: *covers the theoretical elements of 'who' you are and 'why' you are. It helps you to see how you create you perceptions and how they affect your life.*

Part Three: *offers practical tools and techniques for applying lasting changes to your life. Use a combination of techniques to come up with your own recipe for creating your ideal life.*

Throughout the book, each chapter is in a three-part format, beginning with a short story as a metaphor for the underlying principle that follows.

Metaphors and stories are effective in bypassing the objections of your conscious mind. They help relate a concept in an indirect manner that overrides conscious objection.

Stories also ease your mind into a state of relaxation where you will be more receptive to the content that follows.

Following the short story, the broader concept expands in more detail and the last section of each chapter offers tools, applications and references on how you can apply the principles.

Your own story starts now.

Visualise yourself standing in a field.
In front of you is a thick forest and treacherous mountains.
Where you are standing, you look around and can see your existing world around you. You can see your challenges and problems.

On the other side of those mountains is your own personal 'Utopia'; a world where you have the power to create and change anything you want, exactly as you want it to be.

Look towards the forest. A giant walks out from a small track in front of you. As you look up into his giant face, he smiles at you and speaks.

'Have you ever noticed that sometimes magical things just happen?'

'Have you ever thought of someone and then the phone rings that very instant?'

'Have you ever had a moment that seemed oddly familiar? A De Je Vu?'

The giant says with a nod, 'You're a wizard!' ….Ok, I might have borrowed that concept from JK Rowling, but I do it only to illustrate a point.

In the books we read, secondary characters have the same 'abilities' as the hero but the hero will usually have one distinct advantage. The hero is told that he is special. He believes the prophecy of 'what could be' and through the adventure he becomes 'what is'.

Everybody is unique and born into different circumstances. We each have our own view of the world and have different experiences. The hero didn't know he was special until someone told him. As the co-author of your new adventure, I am telling you now that you are special. Do something with it!

Who Forgot the Tent Pegs?

Some Quick Packing and a Spare Pair of Undies

Before we get started...

We all know that the 'Journey of a Thousand Miles' starts with a single step...but it's still a good idea to pack first.

Quite often I'll been reading a wonderful personal development or business planning book and as I'm sitting on the beach, having a relaxing read, the author says 'Put the book down and go and do this task'.

I get a little bit frustrated because I am reading a book on planning and they have not prepared me for this challenge before I set out for the beach.

Usually I continue reading with the intention of coming back and doing the task when I get home. More often than not, I forget the task and the 'day to day' distracts me from ever coming back to it.

What if that singular task was the one that gave me the insight to make the biggest change in my life? You possibly need to experience the task physically in order to understand the principle behind it. I may have just screwed myself out of an epiphany!

Being the excellent tour guide that I am, before we take the journey to Utopia, I want you to pack. You wouldn't go camping without some basics. You wouldn't go fishing without a fishing rod. Let's get your toolkit ready.

The tools will be most useful in Part Three but I often find it helpful to take notes whenever I read a book.

Whenever you are considering reading this book, always have the following items with you:
- 2 pens in different colours
- A notebook
- An open mind – Some concepts may seem a little abstract. There will be a method behind each concept and I try to keep the explanations as basic as possible.

You are now ready.

Let's go!

PART ONE

PARAMETERS FOR CHANGE

Chapter One

Transmutation Class

Watch me Turn a Rabbit into a Hat!

Chapter One

"My professional life has been a constant record of disillusion, and many things that seem wonderful to most men are the every-day commonplaces of my business."
Harry Houdini

Life was tough for Harvey. Outwardly, he was your typical, run of the mill Martian. He was green, overweight and a little on the hairy side. All in all, nothing really set him apart from his peers.

Harvey worked in a spaceship manufacturing call centre. His days consisted of standing in front of a holographic pod where clients would call and complain about delays in their spaceship delivery or other such menial problems.

Last year Harvey got a little tipsy at end of year party and made out with his boss, Zelda.

He had been fond of Zelda for some time but she was not fond of Harvey. She was drunk and very embarrassed. After the 'incident', she turned into a mega-bitch and made Harvey's life a living hell.

Harvey's team of co-workers were tight and when they saw Zelda starting to ostracise Harvey, they all followed suite for fear of their own jobs.

Harvey had to get out. He dreamed of a great adventure and distant shores and being someone else.

One day after receiving a particularly gruelling session of criticism from Zelda, Harvey made a decision.

He walked into the Senior Manager's office and handed in his resignation. Harvey was going to find another job somewhere else.

Harvey had some savings and decided it was time to make major changes in his life.

He felt confident and unbeatable. He went to the hairdresser, had a shave and a trim, and started to plan for the next stage of his life.

Harvey decided to start afresh. He had heard great things about Saturn and decided to make the big move. He packed up his belongings and was full of confidence. 'I'll never look back,' he thought to himself triumphantly.

His new bungalow was fantastic. It had a spectacular view of Saturn's glorious rings and he was offered a job on the first day when he visited the local ring-surfing shop.

Life was looking up for Harvey, or so it seemed...

Within a few weeks of moving, problems started to surface. His co-workers started gossipping. The roof of his bungalow sprung a leak and everything turned to shit.

Harvey couldn't figure it out. Saturn was no better than Mars. This was supposed to be his fresh start.

He had used up his savings on the move to Saturn and could not afford to quit and start again, so he had to figure out how to make the best of it.

One afternoon, Harvey was passing the local Tarot store when he decided to drop in for a reading. He sat down in front of the clairvoyant and she looked at him with her intense violet eyes. Harvey listened intently.

The clairvoyant spoke, 'I can't give you the answers you're seeking Harvey. I can give you some advice from an old lady. Moving and changing outward situations cannot change what is on the inside. Only you have the answers you are seeking.'

Harvey looked disappointed. The clairvoyant shuffled over to her bookshelf and took a well-thumbed book from the shelf. She handed the book to Harvey.

Harvey looked down at the title 'It's Your Life ~ Your Adventure~ Your Choice.'

(Yep...my book is a bestseller on Saturn!)

Where is your life now?

Are there elements of your life that give you the willies?

Are you happy with some parts and unhappy with others?

Have you read every self-development book under the sun and attended every evangelical seminar you could think of, only to find that you are still you?

Of course, you are still you.

Personal Development and motivational seminars can give you a short-term rush, but they are not a happy pill that will suddenly transform your universe?

The only way to make lasting change is to take action. If you are attending seminars, reading books on self-development, and seeking answers, you are off to a good start but you have to make the commitment to make lasting change.

It is often theorised in politics that leaders aren't voted into office. They are voted out. There is only ever a change of government when the existing government gets it wrong. The same theory translates to making life-changing decisions. Usually change occurs when the existing circumstances are so bad that you can no longer live with them.

I have identified seven parameters for creating long term change:

The first parameter for change is **'Acceptance.'**

Acknowledge and accept yourself as you are and that your life circumstances can change with some effort on your part.

You are perfect in your own skin and your flawed little self can achieve anything anyone else with a pulse has been able to achieve. Beyond physical restrictions and barriers, excuses are just excuses. Some people even overcome their physical barriers to achieve what others would consider impossible.

What you make of your life is a choice, like any other. Accept yourself as you are and either choose to change your life circumstances or accept them as they are. Whining and complaining achieves nothing.

This book can give you some resources and insight but it will not make the changes for you. You need to apply action to implement them. Knowledge holds no value without action.

You must accept that you need to take action to change your life and take responsibility for your decisions.

The second life change parameter is **'Mindset.'**

By having a positive mindset, focusing on the desired outcome and perceiving it as a positive change to both your own and the circumstances of others, you will achieve more.

By talking yourself down or constantly blaming others for your circumstances, you are surrendering your personal power and allowing external elements to dictate your life. You are either the cause or the effect.

Obstacles are lessons. Learn the lesson and move on. Evolve and see the unseen benefits. Sometimes the unseen benefit is a lesson in 'what not to do'. Learning from mistakes is a positive experience and will help you let go and move towards your desired outcome.

The third parameter for change is **'Environment.'**

Everybody needs a sanctuary. Your environment affects your mood as it has the greatest exposure to all five senses - touch, smell, sight, sound and taste. Your environment stimulates all your senses at all times. Your senses respond on an unconscious level.

Making changes to your environment and being aware of its effect on you can be enough to put you in the right frame of mind to achieve more and remove stress.

Many self-development books overlook the external environment as they focus only on the internal shift. You could be doing everything inside to change your outlook and life, but may be unaware of something in your environment that is causing you disharmony.

There are likely reactions and responses within you that you were not even aware existed. Don't give up prematurely.

The fourth parameter for change is **'Communication.'**

Communication is a wonderful gift when you learn to master it on a conscious level. When you focus on communicating clearly and effectively, you will soon realize the power that you hold as a master communicator.

You don't need to be a fluent public speaker or master twelve languages to communicate effectively. Some languages and communication tools are universal. Body language, the tone of your voice and posture play an important role in establishing and maintaining effective communication.

Listening is also a communication tool most of us do not use as well as we should.

Most conflict evolves from miscommunication. One person will say something with an intention that is perfectly clear in their own mind and it can be interpreted a million different ways depending on who is hearing those words.

You are in control of how others hear your message. When you learn to simplify your communication and speak clearly and consciously, you can affect the outcome of any situation by being in control of your actions and responses.

The fifth parameter is **'Fear.'**

Many of our actions and reactions are borne of fear. We have behaviour patterns and habits that have formed over a lifetime that have stemmed from fear of consequence.

Many fears have no logical reasoning. Some of them come from our social conditioning, stories our parents or siblings told us or from physical experiences.

Most fears served a purpose when we were young and learning about our world and our environment, but are no longer relative to our lives as adults. There are many fears we accept and live by as truths. We instil them in our own children and thus the patterns continue.

By consciously recognizing your own fears and seeing how they can hold you back from achieving everything you desire, you can overcome them. You can clear these blocks and create new habits that will serve your purpose in a much healthier and positive way.

Fear can control you but only if you let it. You are the master of your own destiny. If you pay no heed whenever fear arises within you, and overlook it, you take away its power and can move forward.

The sixth parameter for change is **'Commitment and Discipline.'**

Commitment and Discipline - Two words that make most of us wince at the mere thought of them. They both bring images of hard rules, firm regulations, and if you're kinky, perhaps a bit of bondage.

Uttering the word 'commitment' makes, most men think of a ball and chain and most women think of lack.

Speaking the word 'Discipline' conjure images of a cane, forced rules and something we do not like.

Commitment is just a mental shift. You make a decision. You own that decision, and establish it as a part of your identity. It is your own. You commit to wanting a better life that you have clearly defined, and take small steps each day to achieving it and making it a lasting habit.

Discipline is not something that someone else enforces on you. It also does not involve beating yourself up, feeling guilty, giving yourself a whipping or confessing your sins. Discipline is the act of organizing your priorities and time and understanding your personal value system.

When you understand what is most important to you on a deeper level, you can build a personal value system. If you find yourself worrying about things or straying from those values you hold at your core, then discipline is deciding to let go of what is not important and focusing on what is.

Discipline is enjoying the things that are important to you and removing distractions that are not in alignment with who you are and what you want in your life.

The Last Parameter for change is **'Reward.'**

The reason most diets don't work is because they are too rigid. The reason most gym memberships are a waste of money is because we do not reward ourselves along the way.

It's important to give yourself regular rewards to acknowledge that you are achieving and moving forwards. Rewards brings you contentment and joy.

It doesn't matter whether that reward is a walk on the beach, a new pair of shoes, a CD or a plasma TV.

Small rewards inspire us and help us move forward. They strengthen your commitment and give you something external to motivate you.

I will cover each of these parameters more thoroughly in the next few chapters as each plays a significant role in creating the exact circumstances you will need to make an impact in your life.

Think of change parameters as 'setting the mood'. You've got a hottie coming over for dinner. You put on your mood music and dim the lights. The candles are burning. You've cooked mum's secret recipe, and you have had the motor replaced in your vibrating bed…

It's shaping up for a good night!

Chapter Two

Mirror, Mirror on the Wall...

Who are you and What are you Looking at?

Chapter Two

"A friend is someone who understands your past, believes in your future, and accepts you just the way you are."

Anonymous

Once upon a time there lived and evil queen. She was married to a king who was very wealthy, slightly older and nearing death (well he didn't know that but we will cover it as the story progresses). She was very happy that her own smokin' hot exterior had attracted such circumstances to bring her every material joy a sassy wench could desire but she was not entirely content. Something was missing.

The evil queen had a tough exterior. Outwardly she was happy go lucky, had a sharp wit and an equally sharp tongue that she could get away with because she was hot and had lots of money. On the inside though, she was just like everyone else.

Despite all her material joys, she wanted for something but didn't know what it was that she needed to fill the void. She went to hang out with the resident sorcerer to find an answer to her quandary.

Contrary to popular belief, sorcerers were not all mystical and magical like, they were just like modern day nerds; socially inept, often a bit weird and rather than spend all day playing 'World of Warcraft', they would play with their alchemy kits…but I digress.

Marvin was your typical sorcerer, smoke, mirrors, secret crush on smokin' hot queen and eager to impress.

The queen sashayed into his chamber and sat down on his favourite chair. She sighed, 'Marvin, something's missing.'

Marvin had often enjoyed the banter with his queen but had never seen this side of her before. She looked like she might be 'feeling' something. Wow! She had confided in Marvin. Whoa! Marvin fixed his hair and sat next to the queen.

'Well let me know what it is and I'll magic something spectacular,' said Marvin waving his hands around as he magic'd her a glass of red.

'I don't know what it is Marv, that's the problem. I have everything I could want for; money, rich husband, brains and beauty but I still feel like something's missing. How can I find it if I don't know what it is?'

'Oh, I've got just the thing.'

Marvin had been working on a magic mirror.

'All you have to do is stand in front of the mirror and ask it, "Mirror Mirror on the wall, show me my every flaw," I know the rhyme is a bit dodge, but it will show you your true self. It takes balls to do it and I haven't been brave enough but if you're feeling dangerous, it's yours.'

The evil queen took the mirror and every day she stood in front of it, hypnotised and wanting to chant the magic words, but standing only silently. She did not have the courage to ask. What would she see?

Finally, one day, she had a few reds, got a bit tipsy and mustered up the courage to say the magic words.

She squeezed her eyes shut and stood in front of the mirror. She took a deep breath and uttered the words that she had played repeatedly in her mind so many times.

'Mirror mirror on the wall, show me my every flaw.'

A few moments of silence passed.

Slowly, she opened her eyes and looked up at the mirror.

She recognised herself in the mirror but the image staring back at her was not what she expected.

In it, she could see her vulnerabilities, her insecurities, her nakedness, her envy, her confusion, her wants and desires, her stupidity and her conformity.

She had expected to see an ugly hag. She had been playing the role of evil queen and doing everything that one would expect of an ice goddess for quite some time. What she saw was the opposite.

In front of her was the most radiant version of herself that she had ever seen. Her skin was like porcelain. Her hair was like silk and the flaws only made her more beautiful.

The mirror spoke to her without words.

'It's our flaws that make us beautiful.' She had been fitting into an ideal, going against who she was, and living in the expectations of others. She chose this for herself, but she also had the choice to change it and be true to who she was.

Being true to herself meant embracing those insecurities and those flaws and accepting them as a part of herself and having the courage to follow the path of her own choosing.

The queen had been slipping the king a bit of arsenic over the last couple of months because she'd thought that might give her a way out. Instead of knocking him off, she decided it was time to move on and live the quiet life on a farm in the country.

High on her mission, she waltzed up to the king's chamber where he was indulging in kingly pursuits. She announced her departure, packed a bag of her favourite belongings and made her way to the stables.

She put her saddlebag on a little silver horse, made her way down the road, took a few turns here and there following her intuition and smiling to herself. She had no idea where she would end up or who she would end up with? She had decided to take each day at a time and just experience life.

I was the evil queen in this little story. For the record, I was not exactly evil, and I was not slipping anyone arsenic. I just added a bit of poetic license to spice it up a bit.

Unlike the Queen, my country path was not exactly smooth. I crossed a couple of ravines. I met some snakes along the way but I am still here and I am happy with the choices I have made.

When you are planning your ideal life, you need to see yourself through the eyes of the people who love and cherish you. When you ask your mum what she loves about you, you will probably find that it is not what you expected.

When you ask each of your loved ones why they love you, they will each give you a different answer. You need to accept yourself as you are and take responsibility for all the choices you have made.

If you have let someone else control you, or your finances or outcomes, realise that it was your choice to allow it to happen and decide to take steps to fix any problems and stop them from happening again.

Other people do not make you feel the way you do. Only you have the power to command your emotions. It sounds a little harsh, but you really are in complete control over how you choose to feel.

Consider the next metaphor to illustrate this concept.

When you see a rose, it might invoke feelings of euphoria. The smell of the rose, the look and colour of the rose and the touch and feel of the rose all stimulate emotional responses. Most people feel pleasant when they see a rose. Sometimes you don't even need to see the rose; just the word brings feelings of love and happiness.

When another person sees a rose, that person may see the thorns. They may have lost a loved one to gangrene from a rose thorn.

We all perceive others and circumstances using our own filter system based on our own life experiences.

The rose has not done anything differently to invoke those feelings in either of the people receiving it. It is simply a rose being a rose, but one person will see it as a good thing and another a bad.

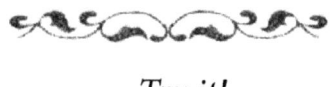

Try it!

When you are confronted with another person or a conflict, separate yourself from the scenario and picture yourself as if you were watching a movie, and consider that that person is just a rose being a rose.

Their behaviour stems from their experiences for that day, their life experiences and their internal belief system.

In your view, and based on your own filters, you may perceive it as right or wrong, but that is irrelevant. That is only your perception and you have control on how or if it will affect you.

This is important. When you are doing the exercises in this book, avoid the habit of casting judgments on yourself or others. When you can be ruthlessly honest with yourself, you can achieve more.

When you are planning your ideal, be honest with yourself. If you want money, fame and a big fancy car with a doof doof stereo, write it down. Ask yourself why you want it and if it is what you want, write it down. Pursue it.

There is no right and wrong. There is only perception. Love and hate are the same emotion. They are just opposite ends of the same pole.

Put your critical judgments aside, accept who you are now and change the bits you no longer need.

Chapter Three

It's All in your Head

The Monster Under my Bed

Chapter Three

"I am looking for a lot of men who have an infinite capacity to not know what can't be done."

Henry Ford

The guardrail gave way and fell down to the raging river below. As Scarlett fell forward and towards the edge, a pair of strong masculine arms swept her up. She gasped. Her heart was beating fast and she looked up into the most gentle, green eyes she had ever seen.

She had noticed him working behind the bar last night but had put the thought quickly out of her mind.

'You've got to watch that first step,' he said in his deep, kind voice.

She couldn't speak and just stood there; wrapped in his nameless arms. She was still catching her breath when he leant down and kissed her. Passion was radiating as his warm lips melted into her own.

Every touch made her quiver and wanting for more as his tongue teased her and he nibbled on her lips.

He was a total stranger. It was the middle of the day.

Her mind tried to talk her out of it, but she was lost in a moment of passion that only existed in movies. Here she was, alone on the cliff's edge with this hard body. She surrendered completely.

He stopped kissing her and stepped back.

She drank him up with her eyes. He was taller than she was, and wouldn't be more than 25. She smirked. His arms were muscular and his mocha skin complimented his knowing smile. Her eyes moved over his body. She scanned up, met his eyes and raised one eyebrow, smiling in approval.

He moved towards her. His strong hands pulled her shirt loose and made their way across the small of her back as he moved her shirt up and over her head.

As he took her shirt off, he kissed her neck and made his way down to her breasts. His hands were already caressing her and making her shudder again. She knew this wasn't the first time he had pulled this move on one of the guests, but she didn't care. It was divine.

His hands expertly explored her body and she moaned.

He lay her down in the grass and he kissed her flat stomach.

Her hands were having an adventure of their own, exploring every inch of his eager body. She felt like a goddess as he worked her body and she teased his mercilessly with her tongue. He pinned her hands down in the soft grass and her body arched in anticipation.

Suddenly her attention was shaken when she heard a thundering grumble. It seemed to come from the same place her head was resting.

She sat up, startled from her ecstasy.

She blinked her eyes and looked around. There was no cliff or handsome stranger but only her husband's hairy back rising and falling as he sniffed, farted and rolled over.

'Mornin' love. Dreaming about Heathcliff again?'

Dammit…

Ahem. Should I give you a moment? If you've had one of 'those' dreams, you will know that when your mind experiences something, the physical output of your body responds as if it were actually occurring.

Olympians often use visualisation exercises as part of their training with the same effect. Their body doesn't know the difference between the real and imagined. Mindset works on many levels.

Henry Ford acknowledged mindset as the most fundamental necessity for success in anything. Another famous quote of his is:

> *"If you think you can do a thing or think you can't do a thing, you're right."*

In stock trading, you'll find every good book on trading will have section dedicated to mindset and discipline.

Many people go into trading to make their fortunes and want to learn the charting and technical elements. They often skip this chapter, but this is the most important part of trading, investing and life planning; in fact, any activity you undertake.

Having the right mindset from the outset will help you plan the rest of your journey. Commit to it and love it and the rest will follow.

You have heard the 'glass half full' analogy. The power of positive mindset may sound all new age, but it does hold true in its simplest form that if you feel inspired, you achieve more.

If you have identified yourself as either an 'away from' person or a 'towards to' person, try not to 'identify' with either.

When you identify yourself as a type or give yourself a label, it becomes a part of your identity. Separate yourself from the behaviour and see it as something that can change.

Does your *'behaviour'* presently move away from things you perceive as negative, or does your *'behaviour'* go towards anticipated outcomes?

If you were demonstrating and 'away' from behaviour, choose to change it. Towards behaviours, achieve more.

The power of mindset lies in the emotions and feelings that it can evoke.

When you set a goal, and focus on the expected outcome, notice how your body's physiology changes. Notice how your heart beats faster and you feel inspired.

When setting goals, ask yourself 'why' you want it. Break it down and be specific. If your goal is to have more money, how much money do you want? Why do you want it? It will likely be for 'security' or a basic and powerful human need.

Once you know why you want it, you can now experience the same feelings you will have when you have achieved that outcome. This will in turn inspire you to move towards your desires and make the mind shift on an unconscious level.

When you set out your plans, a hindrance to achieving the correct mindset is your past or present social environment. I will touch on it briefly here but will cover it in more depth in later chapters.

Often we associate the want for financial gain with guilt or greed and therefore keep our desires private and locked away or feel guilty when they start to come into our life.

Do not reject your desires. Do not feel guilty or play the martyr because you have made the changes to bring wealth into your life. Change your perception of those desires as a 'good' thing. Change the label.

As social creatures, we worry about the judgments of others. We want to be accepted. We want to be a 'good' person. When you focus on the positives of having financial success or personal success, you will want for it without judgment.

If we can think of how our personal success can help others, this will open your mind to new possibilities.

We are often our own worst judges, and much of what we perceive is just imagination at play.

Our self-talk will say, 'They will say this about me. I will be judged as a...' You do not know that. It has not happened yet. It is your imagination. Your imagination often projects into a future that has not yet occurred.

Change your perception of events and anxieties. Do a little contingency planning and decide on some positive responses you might have if it should occur and then let it go.

Your mindset will determine the success or failure of your outcomes. You will achieve all that you can if you believe you can and *allow it to happen.*

Have you heard of people who win the lottery only to be broke just one year down the track? They did not think they were worthy of that wealth. It may take some time for your existing barriers and thoughts to expand to allow your reality to change.

Try It!

In the Seventies, Richard Bandler and John Grinder took concepts from several methodologies and philosophies and created systemised processes for modelling success using language and personal re-patterning and they called it Neuro Linguistic Programming.

I use many of these and similar applications and techniques throughout my book.

One methodology is 'Outcome Thinking'. When you affix your mind to the desired outcome, and work backwards from there, you can change your perception of it becoming your reality.

When you are setting your goals and outcomes, go for gold, set you absolute desires, and work backwards from there.

You will find there are small steps along the way. As you progress and achieve each step, your mindset will expand to the new circumstances and allow the next level of the goal to fit into your new life.

Your mindset grows as your circumstances expand. What may have seemed impossible for your previous mindset will now seem achievable as you have moved closer and accomplished some smaller steps in the direction of your desired outcome.

You will not go from here to there without taking small steps. Have you ever learned something from scratch? You took small steps.

I am sure Jimi Hendrix did not wake up one morning and just know how to play the way he did. He took small steps, and practiced every day and as he learned more, he knew he was capable of more.

Your mindset will evolve and grow. It does not need to be fixed and locked in. It needs to be flexible to allow your outcomes to grow and evolve with you.

Being conscious of your thoughts is enough to set the foundation to real change. A solid foundation is the most important part of a great building. Great change builds upon on a solid mindset.

Chapter Four

The Teddy Bears' Picnic

Do you have a Sanctuary?

Chapter Four

"It's the vibe of the thing, your Honour."

Dennis Denuto – From the Film 'The Castle'

'You are a love machine. You are hot baby. You're going to get a second date.'

Nigel was getting ready for his big date. He had never made it past a first date, and didn't seem to have much luck with the ladies.

He didn't get it. They always said yes when he asked them out. He was good looking and charismatic and confident and he always came up with something imaginative to do. He wasn't one of those boring dinner and movie types.

He was looking sharp in his purple velvet tracksuit. He rubbed one final dash of Brylcreem through his hair and jumped into his Monaro. He cranked the stereo and sped off to pick up his date.

As he was driving up her street, he was noting the swanky houses. She was totally his type. This chick was going to L O V E him.

He had organised the best first date. She sat in the passenger seat, and Nigel decided to set the mood. He politely ejected his Metallica CD and put on Poison. Chicks dig Poison.

The sultry seductions of 'Unskinny Bop' was working its charms on his date, when he pulled into the driveway of a large industrial shed.

'These cage fights are invitation only. They're illegal and totally exclusive. I had to pay premium price to get us in here tonight.' She looked shocked.

'You've got to have connections to get into these things babe. Stick with me and you'll be safe.' He winked at her and mistook her stunned silence for awe.

They walked in through the side door and the smell of sweat, body odour and stale beer was overwhelming. She looked down at her cotton dress and felt a little overdressed.

A biker walked past and grabbed her arse. Nigel stepped in and saw the opportunity to put his arm around her and pull her closer.

He had that one pre-planned. He was THE MAN!

Nigel found them a great seat up front. His date was too terrified to go to the toilet when she started feeling ill halfway through the first fight. She lent over and threw up on Nigel's velvet tracksuit. He was mortified. Nigel suggested they end the date early and took her home.

At least this time it wasn't his fault that there was no second date. Throwing up on your date; he felt so embarrassed for her.

If your environment is stale, it can help to go somewhere else to clear your head. For long-term benefits though, everyone needs his or her own sanctuary.

Ideally, this should be your home - The one place that reflects your personality and brings you peace and contentment.

Your home is somewhere that you can feel safe and be yourself. A home is somewhere you can relax and unwind. A home is somewhere your friends will want to come and enjoy your company.

Think about your work environment. Is it comfortable?

Think about your home environment. Is it safe and calm?

Think about your senses when you focus on images of those environments. Are there any sources of any discomfort?

If you are not at peace when you go home, you can identify what elements are causing that dis-ease and what senses are affected. I used the word 'dis-ease' because this is what will occur when your home or your environment are not in harmony with your values and intent.

Your environment stimulates several of your senses at any given time.
- Offensive smells can cause disharmony.
- Visual clutter can create a feeling of tension and reflect as a clutter in your life. A flickering light can give you a headache.
- Loud music, raised voices and ignorant neighbours starting their truck at 4am in the morning can cause tension and stress.
- Often smells and situations can also leave 'a bad taste in your mouth'.
- Dust and mould can affect your health when you touch them or ingest them.

Your environment affects all of your senses and will have an individual 'energy' too.

Have you ever walked into a room after someone has had an argument? You were not present for the argument however, there is still tension energy in the room. The next time you have a visitor in your home, observe them.

Do people visit your home and feel relaxed and calm?

If your friends cannot enjoy your company in your home, perhaps you can look at ways to change some of the elements.

Notice what senses are affected and what the trigger or cause of those tensions are.

Become aware of your workplace and what causes you stress. There have been endless studies on the layout of offices. The management of a workplace will usually make a judgement call and choose between ergonomics (the comfort and health of the environment for its staff) and budget.

Studies have shown that the popular 'work pod' arrangement of offices; often called a 'battery hen' arrangement; results in decreased productivity, increased sick leave and stress of the workers.

Environmental factors such as natural lighting or simulated natural lighting, having live plants as well as a muted colour scheme can increase productivity.

Your environment can also include the clothes your wear. Colours affect our moods.

If you wear a red dress, you will feel confident.
If you wear green, you will feel calm.
Restaurants paint the walls red or orange, as these colours stimulate appetite.

- *'Energetic'* Colours are those associated with warmth – Red, Orange, Yellow – They stimulate and give you a feeling of energy and fire.
- *'Cool'* Colours – Blue, Green and purple –are calming and associated with peace, water, and health.

Whilst red walls in the bedroom might make for a passionate love life, it will also stimulate anger with the right catalyst and it will not create a calming restful environment.

Green is a good colour for a bedroom as it invokes a feeling of calm and restfulness. It is the colour of trees and nature and can trigger the senses associated with nature.

If your home is not your sanctuary yet, don't stress. As you regain your strength and move forward towards positive changes in your life, you will feel more confident in making any changes that you need to make so that your sanctuary is in line with your new vision.

When you create an harmonious environment, you will notice people are attracted to you. They will want to spend time in your home.

Most people are not aware of their surroundings and the effect they have on their senses. In a peaceful environment, people will leave you feeling energised and calm.

The Australian film 'The Castle' struck a chord with so many people because it defined what a home should be.

Dale Kerrigan sums it up perfectly, *'It's not just a house. It's our home!'*

Try it!

Be conscious of your physical surroundings and note changes you can make to stimulate your senses in a more harmonious way.

If your home is not a sanctuary, and you are not yet in a position to change that situation, make sure you have an escape or somewhere you can go to where you can rejuvenate and find peace.

Somewhere in nature such as a garden or a beach will help calm your senses and bring you back into a place of calmness and peace where you can escape any conflicts in your life even if only for a moment.

Everyone needs a break, a sanctuary and a place to call their own. Without a place of calm that we can visit; even if only in our heads; we feel trapped by our physical surroundings and fall into a 'victim' mentality.

Find an environment that brings you strength. This is your special place and the place where you can find your bearings.

Make small changes and be aware of how your environment affects you so that when you do start applying all the other principles in this book, your environment will be in harmony with your new life circumstances and will evolve with you.

Chapter Five

WT R U TRI N 2 SY

Communicating Effectively can

Influence your Outcomes

Chapter Five

"$DO || ! $DO ; try
try: command not found"

www.thinkgeek.com code for *"Do or Do Not. There is No Try"* - Yoda

In 1976, a man hiked out into the wilderness and started living in a cave. Each day he would leave the cave, sit on a rock overlooking the valley, and never speak a word. He would meditate and look out into the distance.

He stopped shaving, grew his beard and hair long, and wore the same clothes every day.

Soon people started hiking up the mountain to see the man. It was rumoured that he was a mystic and had discovered the wisdom of the ages and it had rendered him silent.

People started bringing tributes to him. Filmmakers made Documentaries about him. He did the same thing for twenty-two years.

At first, he would wander down the mountain to get supplies now and then but when the people started visiting, they brought him supplies and food. Every day, he would just sit on his rock and look out into the distance in silence.

His followers would sit by his side and also look out into the distance and wait. They hoped that some of his wisdom would come to them by being in his presence.

More and more people came and over the years, the stories and rumours evolved.

One day he stepped down from his rock in the middle of the day and looked out over the people who sat before him.

He cleared his throat and everyone looked up in awe.

The air was heavy with anticipation, as he looked around at all the eager eyes upon him. They waited for what seemed to be an eternity until finally he spoke his first words in twenty-two years.

'In October 1976, my wife and I were getting ready to go out to her high school reunion.'

Everyone looked on in silence, as he continued.

'It was then that she asked me the question. It was the one defining question that would dictate the rest of my life.'

The pain was still evident in his eyes.

'I have pondered this question for twenty-two years, trying to find the right answer.'

The old man sighed and went back to his rock and looked silently out over the valley. Everyone waited for him to continue, but he just sat silently on his rock. Tears rolled down his cheek as he continued his silent pondering.
Another year passed and people spoke everywhere. 'What was the question? What was the answer?'
Finally, one day, a young nineteen year old made the trek into the wilderness to see the old man. He sat by his side and spoke to the older man.

'Sir, may I ask you a question?'

The man nodded.

'Sir, will you tell me the question that has plagued you these twenty-three years?'

The old man looked down at the young man and spoke.

'The wrong answer could change your life forever.'

The young man nodded and encouraged him to continue.

The old man continued, 'It seemed like such a harmless question but it changed my life. My wife asked me, "Does my bum look fat in these pants?" Pray you never get asked that question son.'

I once had a friend who was born with his foot in his mouth. If there was any possible way he could unintentionally manage to offend someone, you could guarantee it would come from his mouth.

Communication occurs on so many levels. Much of our communication is assumption based on our own view of the world.

When I was building my website and using an abundance of colourful words to express my woes, a friend of mine sent me the link for a t-shirt with the Yoda quote at the beginning of the chapter. To Average Joe it doesn't make much sense but when delivered to the right audience, it is hilarious. I'm a nerd with a penchant for Star Wars. I laughed aloud when I read it.

How we communicate is one of the most powerful tools we can master. Words have the power to influence entire countries. Words can linger long after you have passed and influence generations beyond your own. Words can infuriate a conflict or calm a savage beast. Words can invoke emotions like nothing else.

A picture can paint a thousand words but a single word can inspire poets, artists, lovers, politicians, sages, writers and children. Think about the word 'love'. Think of the emotions you feel. Think of your past loves. Think of how it can make you feel euphoric or experience the pain of a broken heart.

We use words to communicate on many different levels in any day, but when we speak, do we consciously think of the gravity of how we can affect others?

There is an ongoing argument about teenagers submitting essays in 'text' speak. Some argue that it is a recognised part of society today and we should accept that it is the chosen language of the next generation.

For centuries, language has evolved and changed with each generation. We no longer speaketh in thine olde English tongue and we use common slang words in our daily speech. Words that were once considered obscene are now common and haven't the shock value they were once esteemed.

I remember getting a wallop for saying the word 'bum' when I was little. Now that word is on billboards. It's even deemed as 'cute' in the right context.

The complexities of communication go even further when you include, the tone of the delivery, the inflections of your voice, where you place the emphasis and body language.

Being aware of your purpose and communicating with a desired outcome is the strongest communication skill you can learn and master. When you make a commitment to change, you will need to muster your communications skills to manage some situations that may arise.

As you go through a journey of significant life changes and as you start making more informed and confident choices, many of those around you will still be in their old mindset and mode of thinking and you will need to be aware of this when you are communicating with them.

When confronted with change, some feel challenged or obliged to 'keep up' and you may come up against some aggression. They see you making choices that are not in complete alignment with their own and the base of friendships is rapport and common interests.

You will need to use your communication skills in handling these challenges. In every decision you make, be aware of the other person's filters, beliefs and values.

Their communication style is the outcome of a lifetime of habits and habits can be hard to break. Also consider that in order to break those habits, you have to want to break them or make the choice to take an alternate path.

One of the challenges you will discover is the changes in the attitudes of others when you start being more assertive and saying 'no'. This one is particularly relevant to women. Society grooms us to serve and put everyone else's needs ahead of our own.

Often it is our instinct to say 'yes' when asked to help others. We play the martyr with the intention of helping those around us but I have learned that in doing so, we may not be helping at all. We are robbing that person of a lesson they may need to learn for their own development.

You will find the same people have the same recurring 'problems'. If those around them are offering band-aids every time, that person will not become stronger and more self-sufficient and they will not respect you either.

Obstacles are only negative if you do not learn the lesson. Obstacles are in fact opportunities to grow and evolve. How can you communicate this with another person who cannot see beyond their limited perception?

Whenever someone comes to you with a perceived problem, view it as an obstacle and an opportunity. What would you do if that opportunity were in front of you? What path would you take?

Don't tell them what they should do. It is their journey. Do not take it from them. Tell them what worked for you, guide them and let them make their own choices.

If you presently fix someone's problems all the time, when you take this new perspective, they will feel challenged. That is their choice to make. It is not yours. If they are upset or aggressive, that is their choice to behave that way.

Give others the tools to manage their conflicts themselves, wish them every good fortune and allow them to evolve in their own time. If you take ownership of their problems and make them your own, you are not allowing that person to become all they can be.

Some people enjoy being miserable. Some people enjoy having dramas in their lives. Some people like predictability, even if it is not serving them to their best advantage.

Communicate carefully, effectively, and truthfully with them. Be firm and strong and let them go by on their own journey.

As you go through the various stages of your own development, you will become aware of the many gifts and resources you have. By communicating effectively and with intent and using only positive words and phrases, you will see the snowball effect of how your words can affect and change the world around you.

Be confident when you are speaking. Listen attentively when someone is speaking to you. Two ears and one mouth – use them in that order.

Respect other's opinions and remember you have the choice on whether or not you allow something to affect you.

Occasionally you will meet a chatterbox who will take the ball and run with it. It is fine to be polite and firm and excuse yourself when this happens. Listening attentively should not involve having your ear chewed off.

In no other skill does the law of reciprocity work more effectively than it does in the mastering of communication skills.

The law of reciprocity has many faces. Some call it karma. Some use the phrase, 'What goes around, comes around.' The bible says, 'Do unto others as you would have them do unto you.' Mum might have said to treat others, as you would like to be treated.

I have read a platitude of religious texts and the one core value that is consistent in every one is the universal law. It's called the Golden Rule.

We are all part of a greater whole. We all have our own core values and belief systems but instinctively, we all want respect. It is the simplest formula to live by, but one that is so often overlooked.

Using your words consciously can influence outcomes and create a flow on effect.

For example, one of the life philosophies I live by is a quote by Ghandi:

"Be the change you want to see in the world."

These are some of the most inspiring and true words I have ever heard.

My year two teacher Miss Kelly would say, 'Don't come to me with a problem unless you have an alternative, preferably two.' It worked. I have lived this habit my whole life since.

Using words effectively can influence how your children will grow, it can sway opinions, and it can invoke emotions that influence change.

Hindsight is a wonderful thing.

If you're anything like me, sometimes you say words before you've thunk them. Yes, I know thunk is not a word but it has a "thud' sound to it. That is how my words sound (especially after a red or two).

Later as you go over a situation that you could have handled better, replay it in your mind. If you can call someone, you have offended or apologise and negotiate a better outcome, swallow your pride and make the choice to communicate more effectively.

It will have a better long-term benefit.

There are some groups for men that use some processes to help men learn to communicate better and manage their lives.

One such group has a three day camp of secret mens' business, where men go up a mountain angry and confused. They come down and they are calm and thoughtful and have found an inner peace.

It is an amazing transformation. Some men have a lasting lifelong change. When someone I knew came down from that mountain, he called together his staff for a speech that was one of the most honest and touching speeches I have ever heard.

He had previously not handled his temper or aggression very well and as he spoke to his work colleagues, he said one thing that still resonates with me.

'I know I have not handled situations well in the past. I cannot apologise for my actions as I dealt with those situations with the tools I had at the time.'

He was calm and thoughtful as he delivered his speech. He had made a choice to use the new tools and acknowledge his choices in the past. He was putting his pride aside to correct and remedy any impact those previous choices had had on those around him. This is the essence of courage. He had learned how to communicate his intentions and his words had meaning.

Sometimes it is hard to stay focused on monumental change. Sometimes we fall back into old patterns of behaviour. Be conscious of what you are trying to communicate and speak your words with intention.

Be aware of what you are trying to say. Be aware of how you say it and whom you say it to and you can be the change you want to see in the world.

Try It!

You can apply effective communication in every exchange you have. When you ask for help from another person, ask from his or her perspective.

When someone is angry or upset with you, how would you like him or her to deal with you, if you were in his or her shoes?

Kindness can be disarming. Sometimes the child most in need of praise and love is the one who least deserves it.

You don't know what someone's day has delivered. You don't know why they are behaving the way they are, but you can control the outcome of where the conversation goes from there.

You can make a positive change and a positive experience out of the most heated conflict if you do it with a positive intent on how you would like others to communicate with if you were in their position.

Chapter Six

It was a Dark and Stormy Night

Are you Scared?

Chapter Six

"Audentis fortuna juvet."
"Fortune favours the brave."

Virgil (A. 10.284)

'It's so high mummy.'

Mamma bird gave Midget a nudge towards the edge of the nest.
'Please mummy. I'm scared.' Midget had a tear in his little eye and Mamma tried to be tough.
'You must learn to fly Midget. All your brothers and sisters are flying.' She gave him another nudge.
'Please Mamma. I am scared. I just can't fly.'
Every day for two weeks, Mamma would try to get Midget to fly. He would not even try. Fear paralysed his wings. He just could not take that step off the edge.
Soon the seasons changed and Midget couldn't fly with the other birds. Mamma and the others flew the nest to the ground where Midget could forage for food and be safe.
Mamma cuddled her dear son to her breast and a tear fell on his little head. 'Midget, I must go now. I will see you in the new season. Being a walking bird will bring with it some more challenges. You must not live in fear or you will not survive.'
Midget looked up to the sky as his Mamma, brothers and sisters flew off. That night he slept in his nest in a hollow in the old tree.
He learned that being a walking bird had many other dangers. He managed them as they came but nothing scared him more than flying.
Every day he would make his way up to a low slung branch and stand on the edge willing himself to take the leap and fly, but he just couldn't do it.
He was so afraid. He was going to be a walking bird forever.

Often Midget would look up to the skies awaiting the return of his brothers and sisters.

Soon, the seasons changed again and his Mamma, brothers, and sisters returned. They were grown now and preparing for families of their own.

Midget looked up to the treetops and his heart sank. He could not sing to the other birds. He couldn't have a family of his own. Nobody wanted to be with the walking bird. Midget was so lonely.

One day as Midget was standing on his low branch willing himself to fly, he heard a loud crack above and before him fell the most beautiful bird he had ever seen.

A cat had knocked her off her branch and she had a broken wing.

Her name was Twitter. Midget carried her back to his nest and helped her heal. He brought her grubs and nuts and soon she was healthy again.

When her wing had healed, she longed to fly again and Midget grew sad. He knew that once she flew off, he would be alone again.

As he stood on his low branch and looked up at the other birds, he heard a voice speak to him from below.

'Midget, I can help you learn to fly.'

Midget looked towards the voice.

'Down here,' said the voice.

Midget looked underneath his branch and there was a spider.

Twitter had spoken to the spider and told her Midgets story. Twitter loved Midget and wanted to be with him but he had to learn to fly so he could stay with their family.

The spider told Midget that she would build a strong web underneath his branch and it would catch him if he fell. What a splendid idea!

All night the spider slaved away at her web. Midget was so excited. He could barely sleep.

The next morning, Midget made his way to his low branch and there beneath it was the most spectacular web.

Twitter told Midget what to do. Midget looked up and saw his Mamma, brothers, and sisters all waiting with encouragement. He looked down at the strong web and he wasn't scared anymore.

Midget stepped towards the edge and closed his eyes. He flapped his wings as he stepped off the edge. The wind whistled by as he started to fall but then it happened…A gust lifted him up into the sky.

He flapped with all his might and flew higher and higher and higher.

He was free.

Franklin Delano Roosevelt summed it up beautifully in his first inaugural address:

'Let me assert my firm belief that the only thing we have to fear is fear itself -- nameless, unreasoning, unjustified terror which paralyses needed efforts to convert retreat into advance.'

What is fear? My Collins dictionary defines it as this:

"Fear: a feeling of distress, apprehension, or alarm caused by impending danger, pain etc."

Fear is that feeling you have when you are confronted with a threat; whether it be imagined or real; past, present or in the future. When your heart starts racing, sometimes tears form and you want to flee or avoid a situation, you are expressing fear. When confronted with an unfamiliar situation, our natural instinct will be 'fight or flight'.

If you burned your hand on the hotplate as a child, you learnt not to touch the hotplate because it hurt. This is not fear. This is a learning experience.

If however, someone pushed your hand onto the hotplate, you may have a reaction whenever you go near a hotplate because of that past trauma. This is a 'fear'.

Throughout our lives, we develop patterns and habits. Patterns and habits are changeable. Fear can become a habitual behaviour and we can instinctively react rather than consciously respond to situations.

Sometimes fears come from life experiences that resulted in a trauma. ie: falling off a cliff and hurting yourself. It may result in a fear of heights but that fear is no longer relevant as an adult who has learned from the past error. Fear stemming from physical injury or trauma can be harder to shake but the most common fears come from other people or social and media influences.

Some of your instinctive reactions are from past situations and no longer have any bearing on your present state. Imposed on us at a young age, during our 'imprinting' stage most of our fears come from choices of an authority figure.

Some common fears that we have that are from our social conditioning and external stimuli might be a fear of spiders, a fear of snakes, a fear of heights, a fear of public speaking, a fear of ridicule or even a fear of success.

What we fear is different for every person. For some of us, it is a fear of failure but for most of us, it is actually a fear of success. Failure is manageable. Failure gives us an excuse not to try again. Fear of success however, is an entirely different scenario.

It is commonly spoken that once an object is in motion it tends to stay in motion. Success can have a snowball effect and the thought of this within our present mental limitations can instil the fear of losing control.

There is only a limited way we can manage the outcomes of a large-scale success or action in motion and that is with our communication skills.

Quite often, the fear of the outcome is an imagined scenario. It has not occurred yet and fear can block you from achieving and following your bliss.

The first step to overcoming fear is to take a small step 'towards'.

My small step was to set myself the challenge of writing a book in a single day. I did not achieve it in a single day, but I have been carrying this book around in my brain and anticipating it for 2 years without any action.

I decided on Wednesday, that the time for me to write this book is now and I set aside Sunday to sit down and write until I could write no more.

So, task in hand, I sat, down in front of my computer and the thoughts starting churning...'What if? What if? What if?' I imagined those fears as a mist, I let them drift off, and I started writing.

Firstly, I made the situation one that was comfortable. I made it familiar. I started writing as if I was speaking to one of my friends or family. I started writing with the intent that I will reach someone, somewhere in this world and make his or her world a better place, and with that intention, I have overcome my personal fear. I broke it down into a manageable concept.

I decided I was not writing for a larger population. I was speaking to one person only. It didn't seem so daunting in that perspective.

It doesn't matter what your fear is. The first step is the hardest. Take that step even if it is just a baby step. Have the courage.

Try It!

One way of managing fear is to acknowledge the fear as if it were a separate entity outside of yourself. See it coming towards you and let it drift and pass right through you as if it were a mist.

This is a visual exercise. It will acknowledge the fear exists. However, it is not a part of your identity unless you allow it to be so. You have acknowledged it and chosen to let it pass.

You will find you don't even need courage if you change your perception of situations that stimulate the feelings of fear within you. Break the situation down into something smaller and familiar and work your way up from there.

Most fears are in the future. The future has not happened yet. You cannot predict the outcome so let it be and focus on the existing moment and your presence in the 'now'. When you have cleared your mind of any distractions and let any thoughts or anxiety drift away. Take that first step.

Don't live by the 'shoulds' and 'coulds'.
Live by the 'wills' and 'dos'.
Eliminate the words 'should' and 'could' from your vocabulary.
Don't be a 'Talky'. Be a 'Doey'.
Actions speak louder than words.

Chapter Seven

How Strong is your Resolve?

Does the word Commitment make you freak out?

Chapter Seven

"If it is to be, it is up to me."

William Johnson

'I've invented something.'

'Really?'

Carrie sat down and listened to the professor's latest invention. He rolled out the blueprint and it was obvious that he had been up all night working on this latest scheme.

This latest invention was a helmet that reads your thoughts and sends an instant message to your friend's helmets.

He not only had blueprints, he'd built some.

The professor ran off to the laboratory and came back out wearing a bicycle helmet with gadgets and springs protruding from every orifice.

'Here put this one on Carrie.'

The professor handed her an identical helmet and she put it on her head. Immediately her brain started seeing images of all sorts of ridiculous inventions. The Professor's mind was in overdrive and sending her image after image. She took the helmet off and smiled.

The professor had a new scheme or invention every week. She sat through every one of them, as she loved the dear man. Some of his inventions were nothing short of brilliant, but he would never finish one before he was onto the next. He would go off on a tangent and start excitedly telling her about this latest invention. It was going to change the world.

The same conversation would always eventuate.

'So professor, what are you going to do now?'

'How much have you done on your project?'

'Is it nearing completion?' Carrie would ask.

'Oh Carrie, I'm just working on this new invention I've got. I'll have to get back to that other project another time.' He would say.

Carrie looked around the Professor's workshop. There were gadgets, gizmos, and whatsits everywhere the eye could see. After another exhaustive demonstration, Carrie went home for the night.

That evening, the Professor had a car accident, his life gone in an instant.

Carrie wrote the Professor's eulogy. The professor had a small group of friends and wasn't well known. Carrie looked around at the small gathering and read out her eulogy. It was just 2 sentences.

'My dear Professor was the greatest mind who ever lived. Since I was a little girl, he has inspired me and awed me with his brilliance but nobody knows it.'

Everyone knew it was true. The professor was a brilliance forgotten.

Do you get easily distracted? Are you full of good intentions but lack follow through? Do your friends joke that you're scatterbrained?

I have caught myself procrastinating or making excuses for lack in my life. That's in the past now. *Poof* Gone!

I committed to making positive changes in my life and sometimes I do need to be hard on myself and force myself to stay focused, but when I see the outcome of my work, I know it is worthwhile.

Commitment can become a part of your identity. When you say you are going to do something, others can be sure that it is a commitment.

When you have made it a part of your identity, if you are late for an appointment, you won't need to make an excuse. You won't make any excuses for anything anymore.

If you are running late, others will know it was because you had a higher priority or it was for a valid reason. You do not need to justify your actions. Having commitment as strength of character and living it in action, results in respect from others.

When you spend time with someone, they know their time is valuable and you respect them. Why? Because you are committed to your personal values. You own your commitment and demonstrate it through action.

When you make the shift to committing yourself to a purpose, situation or other person, you have to live that commitment and be true to your word.

Commitment and honesty are the same.

Committing to change is not a painful exercise. It is an act of self. You will need to outline your agenda clearly and know what your desired outcomes are. I will give you some tools for doing this in later chapters.

The more specific you are in your desires, the more easily you will live those values and commitment will become habit for you.

By saying, 'I commit to having a better life', you are not committing to anything. Everyone's perception of a 'better' life will be different. How, specifically will you be committing to that life? Will you be making lifestyle changes and watching your health? Will you be improving your financial situation by learning about stock trading?

Those are specific actions. Within those actions and agendas will be other actions and agendas.

The same can be said for commitment when you look at it in its most common interpretation – that of relationships. 'I am going to commit to my girlfriend.' This says nothing when you look at it.

To what exactly are you committing? How and what are you committing? You might be committing your time, or a portion of it. You might be committing that time with another girlfriend too. Be specific.

Be firm in your convictions. It is easy to demonstrate your commitments and convictions when you associate only in your present moment.

Over our lifetimes, western society teaches us to live in the past or the future. All we have at this exact moment is this moment. Enjoy the moment you are in now.

Think about it. If you have set yourself a daily plan, take each task one at a time. Choose to focus in that moment you are in. You have demonstrated your commitment.

Living in the 'now' and the present has a very real power. Sometimes you find yourself thinking ahead or drifting off with thoughts of what 'needs' to be done or distracting yourself with tasks other than the one in front of you. By allowing this to happen, you are not going to get anything finished and the quality of your output will be less than it would be if you were focusing on the present.

We pride ourselves on multi-tasking. We wear it as a badge of honour.

I have untrained myself how to multi-task. Yes, I can do many things at a time. I can make dinner and watch a movie, help with homework, talk on the phone and write a shopping list all at the same time. Do I get to enjoy any of those activities in that moment? No.

If, however, I focus on one task at a time, I get to enjoy it and give it my full attention. When everyone is used to you doing everything at once, people will have developed expectations and continue to demand more.

By communicating effectively and telling them that you will only do one task at a time, others will learn to adjust to your new pace and will appreciate that your output is much stronger when you live in the moment. They will also appreciate that when you are spending time with them, they will know that you respect them and are giving them your full attention.

Commitment becomes a habit when you focus on the present as a purposeful behaviour. Commitment does not mean you can't be flexible and change your mind. You may find that after committing to something, it may not be what you expected. It may not be for you. This is fine. Commitment allows for flexibility.

Commitment means living in the moment with total clarity and focus. Longer term goals or desires may change. You may find yourself doing a task that you have taken on out of a sense of obligation or guilt.

You may find that when you reassess certain tasks with your personal values, you don't actually want to do that task. That is fine too.

You are not backing down on your commitment; you are acknowledging that it does not serve your higher priority to yourself and values.

Focus on your communication and be firm when you make the commitment not to do things that don't serve your higher contentment.

Discipline and commitment go hand in hand. They are constant companions. Discipline does not work when you use the 'big stick' approach. Discipline is the act of staying true to your values and what brings you joy.

If you find yourself, distracted with tasks or people who do not bring you joy, discipline is the act of letting go of those things that don't serve you and going back to your path, doing things and forming relationships that bring you joy and contentment.

Try It!

Discipline and Commitment can become habits. Habits are repeated patterns of behaviour that become automatic responses.

At first, they will be conscious thoughts and changes, but as you practice them each day and identify with them, they will become a part of who you are and become habitual thought and behaviour patterns.

Look inside yourself. Turn your brain off and listen to your intuition. It will be a whisper at first.

Do what you are supposed to be doing. Everything that will be from thereon is perfect outcome for your intended purpose.

Chapter Eight

Goody Goody Gum Drops

It is Important to Give Yourself Litte Treats

Chapter Eight

"The marvellous richness of human experience would lose something of its rewarding joy if there were no limitations to overcome. The hilltop hour would not be half so wonderful if there were no dark valleys to traverse."

Helen Keller

Chick Chicka Chick Chicka Chick Chicka Chick Chicka Boop Boop Chick Chicka Chick Chicka Chick Chicka Chick Chicka Boop Boop

Lauren had ditched the gym for another round of Commando. If the gym were half as addictive as her Atari 2600, she would have abs like Xena.

Chick Chicka Chick Chicka Chick Chicka Chick Chicka Boop Boop

'Just one more level and I'll be off to bed,' she said to herself. She shot some more baddies and the pace of the music picked up.

'Woo Hoo!' She did a happy dance…another level. She had never gotten this far before. She'd make it to level five. 'Go Champ!'
She had to concentrate and focus. She was going to get all the way to the end this time.

Chick Chicka Chick Chicka Chick Chicka Chick Chicka Boop Boop

In the back of her mind, she had the shits with herself for not going to the gym but she just couldn't pull herself away.

'DAMMIT. Man down.' She had just one life left.

Chick Chicka Chick Chicka Chick Chicka Chick Chicka Boop Boop

She manouvered behind the barrier, ran across the field dodging bullets and 'Pachow! Look out, she's got the big gun now! Sweet, another level.'

She looked down and noticed she was still in her pyjamas from the night before. She'd been playing this thing all day. She laughed and did the new level dance.

'Just one more level. NUTS! Last man down.'

She threw the control on the floor and went to bed.

That night she dreamt of herself at the gym. The gym layout looked like the Commando field. Instead of the upbeat gym music, she could hear the familiar tune of Commando.

Chick Chicka Chick Chicka Chick Chicka Chick Chicka Boop Boop

The Atari version of herself made her way to the step machine.
The Atari version of herself had a huge arse. She needed the step machine.

Chick Chicka Chick Chicka Chick Chicka Chick Chicka Boop Boop

Everything flashed …NEW LEVEL! The plump version of herself did a little jump in the air and a new, slimmer version of herself appeared ready for the next level.

'Oh yeah!'

She worked her way through the Rowing Machine Level and through a session of Body Pump. Now why couldn't the real gym be this fun? Life should be more like Atari.

The levels of a computer game are just long enough to keep you addicted but not so short that you don't have to work for them. At the end, there is usually a reward of some type. Sometimes it's a bonus life, a power sword, or a big bazooka.

Rewards without a cause are empty and the joy of them only lasts a moment whereas when you reward yourself for an effort you have made, that creates a lasting imprint and value on both that item and on your efforts.

For example, if you reward yourself with a pair of shoes; every time someone comments on those shoes, you will feel the same joy you had when you bought them new and you will most likely say 'I bought these as a reward for myself when I finished writing my book,' or whatever achievement you've had.

This is sometimes referred to as an 'anchor' as it creates a stimulus and attaches it or 'anchors' it to an associate point of reference. The benefit of having more rewards for your small victories is that there will be more visual and physical stimuli in your environment to remind you of your achievements and drive you to further achievements.

If you determine how you are going to reward yourself at the onset of starting a project, and commit it to writing, your chances or achieving your outcome is increased.

Sometimes the reward will be the achievement alone. However, even as we achieve and feel the pride and joy that brings, it is always good to anchor those feelings with a token of some sort, be it a glass of red, dinner with friends or a holiday.

Make sure you take the time to reward yourself. Whilst having a firm resolve and powering through your work and commitments with unwavering focus does feel good and inspiring, you do need to take a break occasionally and stop to smell the roses.

There is no point achieving a great feat if you cannot stand back and admire the work. There is no joy in diving from one project to the next. Enjoy the sense of accomplishment that comes with achievement.

The journey is just as important as the destination. It's repeated many times in countless proverbs.

When you are painting, focus on enjoying the act of painting rather than the finished product and it will take care of itself. When you finish; enjoy the finished piece. Relish it, marinade on it, and breathe it in before jumping right into the next. Celebrate and recall the experience.

If you are travelling up a mountain, enjoy the journey. Enjoy the surrounding nature and the wonders it brings but when you get to the top, don't just turn around and go back down. Look on the view in awe of what it is to be alive. Appreciate the blisters on your feet. Breathe the mountain air. Laugh with your companion. Enjoy the moment and the experience and reward yourself for achieving what you have.

I am notorious for working and focusing too hard on what I'm doing and jumping straight into the next project.

I have always rushed about doing everything that needed doing. I have always been juggling. I always have all the balls in the air. Sometimes it feels good to identify myself with doing so much as it makes me feel needed.

When I became aware of my habit for doing this, I had to step back and ask myself why I felt this way and what was lacking.

A good example is relationships. Sometimes we dive into relationships. We rush them along at a pace trying to get somewhere too soon. We don't stop and enjoy the moments. We don't reward ourselves for the little milestones. We don't see the journey because we are too busy focusing on the next one.

We have to get married. We have to have children. We have to have a house.

We are too busy focusing on external factors and obligations and we are not truly rewarding ourselves as we accomplish things along the way.

When you have a child, plan for it and plan for how you will reward yourself. When you have a baby, it is hard work. You may start seeing your time with the baby as work rather than a rewarding experience.

It might be by working from home or taking time off and going to the park every second day. Have a reward. By having a reward, you will also view some activities in a different light.

Try It!

When you buy a new home, you will feel a rush of joy, however, as your mortgage payments come in, you may start to resent it. If you have a reward for yourself that is regular and you associate with that house, you will appreciate it and see it as a part of your overall journey.

You might decide to go to the movies every day the mortgage is due. Rather than associating that day with a mortgage payment, you will associate it with going to the movies – a regular and enjoyable activity that you do together.

Rewards can change our perceptions and can give us an incentive to keep moving forward and not get overwhelmed.

Keep them within budget. Do not create unnecessary stress for yourself by overcommitting your finances. Rewards do not have to be material consumer items. In fact, it can be fun to try to think of as many free rewards as you can.

- A walk on the beach is free.
- Writing a letter to a love one and telling them you love them is free and is rewarding. Getting a real letter in the mail is great.
- Going to the park with your kids is free.
- Time is free if you use it wisely.
- Some councils and community groups put out newsletters and list on their websites free activities for families and singles.
- Smelling a flower is free.
- Listening to music is free.
- Reading a book from the library is free.

As long as it is a reward and you give yourself the time to enjoy your reward, you will continue to strive and achieve. You will see the long-term results of your achievements and feel the joy that brings you.

PART TWO

UNDERSTANDING THE 'WHO'
and 'WHY' OF YOU

Chapter Nine

Pulling Apart a Gadget to see how it Works

Understanding your Perceptions

Chapter Nine

"So, young woman, the way forward is sometimes the way back."

The Wiseman - from the film Labyrinth

From when he was young, John had loved the possibility of creating something that was going to be someone's treasure.

His father was a clock maker. As a boy, he would stay up late by candlelight and watch as his father cast his expert hand over his latest masterpiece. Each piece was a beauty to behold.

His father was renowned worldwide and all who owned on of his pieces treasured it dearly. John had learned his father's artisanship and then went on to forge his own name as the maker of the world's most valuable music boxes. Each music box was a work of art. From the delicate workings of the internal mechanisms to the gold plating and inlay of the wooden casing, he took pride in creating every minute detail.

If an overly keen child broke one of his treasures, John knew exactly how to repair it to bring it back to its former glory. Every cog was perfect. Every part of the final piece had to be precise and perfect for the finished project to bear his name.

To be a true artisan and a master of his profession was a matter of pride. His family name was synonymous with perfection. He could not produce an inferior product or mass-produce his work even though he had the ability and knew how.

After John's lifetime, his music boxes passed from generation to generation. The fine art of creating the boxes soon faded as music boxes gave way to modern technology and soon there were very few artisans left, let alone any to the standard of the great maker himself.

Many years later, a well-meaning husband wanted to change the tune of his wife's treasured music box to 'their' song as a gift for her birthday, so he set about pulling the music box apart. Surely, such antiquated technology could not be that difficult.

He used his best tools and lovingly took apart every small cog, wheel, and join. He dismantled the box looking for the familiar wheel with the pins. He thought it would be a matter of replacing it and having one made with their song…but it was not so with the boxes of the famous maker.

Legend said of the great maker's boxes, that the music came from his soul. No other maker ever figured out where the music came from. The husband was in despair. He had broken his wife's most treasured possession.

He frantically looked up everything he could find on the internet about music boxes and finally came upon a small article about the great maker. As he read of the great maker, he wept. How could he ever fix his wife's treasure if the secret passed with its maker?

The husband spent every moment scrutinising, analysing all the components and trying to remember how it came apart. As he examined every piece he fell in love with the delicacy of its perfection and finally, he put the box back together and he'd discovered the secret.

The husband set the music box on the mantle and never touched it again. He then set about using his new wisdom to create a box of his own. It lacked the finesse of the original but it was functional and built of love.

When he presented it to his wife, the look on her face as she played the box spoke volumes. She knew the story of her own music box and knew that this new box was the product of knowing the absolute intricate knowledge of its predecessor.

Who each of us are is work of art. We are all borne of the palette of our parents and the generations before them and come into this world as pure perfection and a living representation of infinite possibility.

If you asked either of your parents where you came from, you might get a story about a crazy night in dad's Sandman, but even if they relived the moment to perfection, they could not re-create an identical version of you.

As we go through life, we experience various stimuli that mold us and shape our perspectives of the world and our interpretations of what it means. We associate a meaning and a reason to external events and build our value system.

Our value systems and our filters are what make us completely individual in every way. Whilst you may share DNA with an identical twin, there is no way that you will respond and react to the same situation in exactly the same way. Understanding yourself and your reasons for responding the way you do to external factors, is a necessity in creating change on a lasting level.

A large percentage of our responses build on subconscious filters that we are not even aware of and this part of the book will give you an overview of how these filters and belief systems evolve and how you can control them for a more beneficial outcome in the future.

This section is broken down into seven chapters. These cover elements of our fabric that can prevent us from achieving our intent if we are not aware of them.

Social Conditioning covers the unconscious conditioning we experience daily that is constructed on a purposeful level to mold our behaviour. Social Conditioning comes from various sources such as government, culture, media, parents, friends, religion and advertising.

Ego - Our ego is that inner voice that is the projection of who we think we are. Our identity is our view of the ego and ourselves. It comes from our life circumstances, our internal views and opinions, our need to be accepted and our wanting and desires.

Excuses - There are three main excuses for limiting behaviour and not achieving our goals and desires. The excuses we make to ourselves to justify inaction usually hold little weight when they are confronted on a conscious level.

Time Management - How is it that some people get so much done in a day and others seem to be busy all day yet have little to show for it?

Finances - Taking responsibility for your actions, and your finances will give you greater control and understanding of your personal worth. Self-education is the best investment you will ever make when it comes to managing your personal financial situation.

Love and Relationships - What is love? What constitutes a 'good' relationship? Does it exist? Where does it fit in your overall schematic for life?

Managing Life Changing Experiences - Despite our differences on a deeper level, there are some common themes across almost everyone's life. Most major life changing experiences are matters of the heart and impulse decisions. Proper planning and a methodical approach can help with contingency planning when the honeymoon is over and the dust settles.

Chapter Ten

Don't Listen to what the Salesgirl tells you

Orange is not your Colour and she works on Commission

How Many of your Choices are your Own?

Chapter Ten

"Honey, trust me. The Mullet is the new black"

The Hairdresser responsible for the current trend
of haircuts our youth are presently sporting

H owdy Folks. Welcome to today's show.

'Today we're going to be talking to Prince Charming and his new wife Sleepybelle.'

'This is Prince Charming's third marriage.'

'Sleepybelle has asked us to surprise him with his two ex wives, Tressebelle and Snowbelle to shed some light on where he may have gone wrong so their own marriage will truly be 'Happy Ever After.'

'Firstly, let me bring out Prince Charming.'

Dr Bob made his way up to the couches on centre stage and Prince Charming walked across the stage and took a seat next to Dr Bob. Sighs came from the audience and several women swooned at the sight of Prince Charming. He was absolutely gorgeous. With his tanned skin and dark hair, he was every woman's dream.
Prince Charming flashed a broad smile of glistening white teeth at the women in the audience. There were more sighs and more swoons and some women started giggling and blushing like schoolgirls.
He really was quite magnificent.

'Welcome to the show Prince Charming.'

'Thanks Dr Bob. It's great to be here,' he said as he brushed a stray bit of hair from his deep brown eyes. More sighs erupted from the audience.

'Congratulations on your recent marriage. I heard it was a grand affair. You will of course be aware that once the dust settles, there's more to a marriage than elegant dresses and cake.'

'You've been down this track twice before. Do you know what might have gone wrong?' Dr Bob waited for the prince to answer.

'I just don't understand it Dr Bob. I gallop in and sweep these fair maidens off their feet. Sometimes, I even rescue them from a dragon or a tower and after the wedding; it all seems to go downhill.'

Dr Bob intervened. 'How about we bring your new wife out? Who wants to meet Sleepybelle?'

The audience cheered.
Sleepybelle was a beautiful fairytale princess. She had blonde hair down to her waist, ruby red lips and wore the most elegant jewel encrusted gown. She seemed to glide across the stage as she took a seat next to her husband. She sat holding the hand of her beloved.
Before Dr Bob could speak to her though, she rested her head on her husband's shoulder and fell asleep.

'She does that,' laughed the prince as he stroked her hair gently.

Dr Bob laughed and decided to skip ahead and bring out Prince Charming's previous wives.
Tressebelle and Snowbelle were exquisite and graceful. Tressebelle, known for her trademark long blonde hair, had since had her hair cropped into a stylish pixie cut which suited her well.
After parting ways with Prince Charming, she decided to get her Masters Degree in International Business. When it didn't work out between the Prince and his second wife, Snowbelle, Snowbelle had turned to her for guidance and the two found solace in each other's arms.

Chapter Ten - Don't Listen to what the Salesgirl tells you

They sat next to each other in the centre couch. Tressebelle had dispensed of the usual princess attire in favour of a power suit and Snowbelle wore a flowing gown sewn out of spun gold by her fairy godmother.

Bob looked over his guests and addressed Tressebelle first.

'Tressebelle, Could you tell me why you think your marriage to Prince Charming didn't work out?'

'Most definitely,' said Tresse.

'When I was a little girl, I did everything little girls do and was told that one day a prince would save me and I'd live happily ever after. I was locked in a tower, and grew my hair very long so that when he came, he could climb up and take me away into the sunset.'

'After the marriage, I started to question everything I'd been told. I also realised that living happily ever after didn't just happen. In fact, the prince wasn't all that attractive when he wasn't wearing his wig and fine clothes.'

The prince flicked some stray hair from his eye again and blushed. "Ahem...it's not a wig.'

The audience laughed as Tresse continued.

'I had an expectation and the reality of it was quite another thing altogether.'

'Soon after the marriage, we began fighting and realised we both have very different definitions of 'Happily Ever After' and decided to part ways.'

Snowbelle told a similar story. She had been living with seven slovenly roommates when the prince happened across her path. She rode off into the sunset with dreams and visions of her golden future.

She spoke, 'The prince thought that seven was a nice number so decided firmly that I'd bear him seven children.'

'I lived the illusion for eight years, however, seven children back to back takes its toll on your body. I know I wasn't looking my best but it was still heartbreaking to find the prince dancing with a golden haired woman in glass slippers at the annual ball. This was not my idea of "Happily Ever After."'

Since the separation, she'd started her own fitness empire and was looking mighty fine for someone who'd pumped out seven children. The audience cheered loudly and the shine was starting to fade on Prince Charming's smile. Dr Bob intervened, 'Prince Charming, there's two sides to every coin. What's your perspective?'

Prince Charming explained that as a young lad he learned how to be a great fighter, a fine horseman and an excellent dancer. He was not at all surprised when he won on the first season of 'So You Think You Can Dance'. He always knew that one day he would rescue a fine maiden using his swordsmanship. He would take the maiden back to his castle on his stallion and they would dance until dawn on the night of their marriage.

He then assumed his life would be wonderful with such a beauty to share it with, but it was not so. He had geared his whole life to the rescue and the wedding that he did not quite know what to do with himself after that so he just kept rescuing and enjoying the subsequent swoons and affection of every maiden that crossed his path…that is until he met Sleepybelle. He wanted it to work this time. The audience clapped as Prince Charming concluded his woeful tale of debauchery and his true love for Sleepy.

Dr Bob spoke.

'Well folks, that's all we have time for today. Tune in next week as we explore the marriages and our guests lives in further detail. Thanks for joining us today. I'm Dr Bob, please thank our guests, and we'll see you next week.'

Chapter Ten - Don't Listen to what the Salesgirl tells you

The next time you go to an amusement park, take notice of the buildings and set designs. The second and subsequent stories of the buildings are actually half the size of a real building. This is 'forced perspective' and was also a tool also used by the architects who built the facades and cathedrals for the Church.

The Cathedrals were designed is in a manner to make the mortal feel insignificant in the eyes of God. As with much of our social conditioning, many stimuli we are not even aware of has been purposely constructed and presented to fly under the radar.

When you take a step back and break down who you are, what you do and the choices you have made, you will realize how many of those choices are made for you.

There are many assumptions we make, and take for granted as simply the way things are.

Advertising and marketing base their principles on social conditioning and a thorough knowledge of how the human mind works.

A good illustration of conditioning in action is the circus elephant. Have you ever noticed that the circus elephant is tethered by nothing more than a rope and tent peg?

When the elephant was little, he would try to walk away, but he had a rope that was attached to something a lot stronger. Soon he realised that when he had the rope around his leg, he could not walk away so he took it for granted and one day he stopped trying.

The elephant then grows into adulthood and never challenges the tent peg.

How many tent pegs do we have in our lives?

Many of us accept what comes our way and work with it and around it. We do not recognise that we have choices. Everything that is in our lives now is a result of the choices we have made or those made for us in the past.

As adults, we are in a position to make our own choices now. We need to recognise that the barriers to achieving and having what we want are of our own making. Some of the belief systems that served us when we were young are no longer relevant and we can dispose of them in our adult lives.

Our filters and belief systems are unique to our own world and our perception of it. They come from our family, our living circumstances, our life experiences, the society we grow up in, our friends and social circle, the media and the various other people we meet along the way.

You could be living any one of these choices. Choices have been made for you when you were young and you might not even be aware of it. Do any of these sound familiar:

- Work hard and make an honest living.

- Go to university and you'll get a good job.

- The princess kissed the prince and they got married and lived happily ever after.

- Women can have a career, a white wedding, a couple of kids, a picket fence all the while keeping a fantastic figure and going on fun shopping expeditions with your girlfriends where you'll talk about sex and be totally confident and blah blah blah.

Hey, don't feel so bad, I bought into them too. Why not? Some of them are great stories and we want to believe them.

When you look at the amount of choices we make in a day and how many we make on autopilot, you will realise how daunting it can be to really understand the complexity of 'who' you are and 'why' you are.

I am lazy so I just do something very easy to deal with how I make my daily choices. I make a decision in the morning to be conscious of my activities for that day.

I plan my day. What do I hope to achieve today? How am I going to achieve it?

It is a basic exercise in taking ownership of your consciousness. When you are aware of yourself in the current moment, you are less susceptible to conditioning and external influence.

By focusing only on what you can do that day, you bring your awareness internally and it removes the stress of past or future that is not relevant to the 'now'. If I have bills that are unpaid that I cannot afford to pay today, I do not worry about them today.

If you focus on things, like unpaid bills or debts, and build up an anxiety about what 'could' happen, that will be where your focus remains and is counter-productive.

If you focus on doing something positive and achieving something that day, it is a step towards alleviating those longer term problems. Until I am in a position and have the resources to deal with those problems, they are not problems. It is my choice.

This sounds very simplistic, but it works. Many of the problems you have are universal or large problems. They can be cut down to smaller manageable bite size pieces and little tasks you can do in a day.

Now, more than ever, we experience millions of bits of information and stimuli in a day and our minds process it with our filters of importance. Much of those stimuli are deliberately trying to get through your personal filters, stimulate your senses, and thus make your choices for you.

Break your day and tasks into smaller chunks. Pick some of the smaller chunks to do that day and deal with the rest another time. Our 'must have it now' way of viewing the world is just another conditioned response. Reprogram yourself and live your life according to your own terms and conditions.

You cannot save the planet today. You cannot negotiate world peace today. You might have enough money to clear one of your debts today. If that is the case, put it on your list of things to do and look forward to feeling great when it is complete. Only focus on the positive changes you can make today. The rest is irrelevant.

As you become more aware of your emotions and reactions, notice the triggers and ask yourself if your response to that situation is a belief and a choice you have made for yourself.

If it was one made for you, do you wish to keep it or create a new model for your future choices?

If you have committed to your own value system, and if you have experienced the joy that it can bring you to be calm, measured, and take responsibility, then that is now a measure of your values and how you spend your time.

Re-evaluate yourself from time to time and occasionally, if you have strayed from who you are or who you want to be. Choose to go back to where you feel at home and welcome.

You will have people in your life that may inspire feelings of aggression or mistrust or hurt within you. Forgive them. Choose to forgive them. When you forgive and open yourself up to making your own choices, you will be free to be the master of your own destiny.

Forgiveness does not mean you have to like them, it just means letting go and moving on with your own life. If they are a negative person, communicate clearly that you do not want to spend any time with them as your paths are different and wish them well.

Grudges bear the heaviest burden to those who are holding them. Own your choices. By holding a grudge, you are conditioning yourself as a victim and it will not serve your best purpose.

Try It!

Focus only on the present today. Try this exercise.

Imagine yourself standing on a glacier. Picture it as clearly as you can. Notice the cold. Smell the icy air. There is nothing around you for miles. It is a giant glacier.

Consider the unwanted memories of your past as a giant ice shelf overlooking the ocean. You stand safely up on the glacier some distance away from the edge as you look at all the memories, feelings, and emotions trapped inside the ice shelf in the distance.

You hear a thundering crack as the ice shelf breaks away. It bobs up and down a few times and then drifts off into the ocean, never to be seen again taking with it all the past regrets, feeling and memories that you no longer need.

You do not need your past. You have learned the lessons you needed to learn and they are within you. Watch the past drift away and focus on what you have now and where you want to go.

Also, be kinder to yourself.

Chapter Ten - Don't Listen to what the Salesgirl tells you

You have not made any wrong choices. Every choice you have made until now has been the right choice and the right time for you to learn what you needed to know when you needed to know it.

You are now in a position to be the master controller of your life. You are making conscious choices and you are going to do what is best for you.

Choose to be free of judgement.

Choose to love and be kind.

Choose to respond rather than react.

Choose to see the world through rose coloured glasses.

Choose how you feel and what you will be.

Chapter Eleven

Confessions of a Podium Dancer with a Whistle and a Thimble of Dutch Courage

Woot Woot Look at Me!

Chapter Eleven

"Ego: The fallacy whereby a goose thinks he's a swan."

Anonymous

'Don't you know who I am?'

Dave looked patronisingly at the doorman.
The doorman looked embarrassed and let Dave through. 'Haha, worked again.'

Dave packed shelves at the supermarket but when he was not packing shelves, he was a celebrity. He had big dreams. He was one day going to be a famous actor but until then, he was going to live like one anyway. He was not content being Dave the store boy. He was 'Dave the Celebrity'.

He started out by scouring magazine and buying some clothes that looked like the ones the latest celebrities were wearing and saying 'Don't you know who I am?' whenever he was met with any objections.

He was actually quite surprised when he tried it out the first time. His favourite singer was in town and it was rumoured he was going to 'The Mill', which was THE hottest club in town.

He put on one of his new outfits and made his way to 'The Mill'. When he got there, the queue flowed all the way down to the curb.

Therefore, he decided to have a crack at his new theory.

He confidently skipped the queue and tried to assumingly swan pass the doorman. The doorman stopped him and tried to send him back to the end of the queue so he pulled out his new line, 'Don't you know who I am?' whilst looking sufficiently disgusted. The doorman looked confused but Dave was not caving just yet.

He had 'Googled' the club earlier and gotten the club owner's name.

'Just get Sev,' he said haughtily.

The doorman stepped aside and let him through.

'Whew...'

Event after event, Dave tried his routine and nobody asked who he actually was. It was just like the Emperor's new clothes! Soon he began to be an active part of the in-crowd. He had access to a very exclusive group, he always introduced himself as an actor, and eventually he made the right connections and landed his first job.

Funnily enough, the first time he actually had a legitimate reason to be at the studio, was the first time someone asked him, 'Who are you?'

'I'm Dave, the actor,' he said proudly and this time it was true, he had been acting for so long, it felt like a second skin.

Go back to when you were a little kid. Do you remember that feeling when you showed your mum the painting you did at kindy? Mum would have 'ooh'd' and 'aah'd' at your marvel and hung it proudly on the fridge. You swelled with pride, so you went and did another ten paintings to feel it again. That little feeling is your ego.

Our ego is what drives a lot of us to make the choices we make and do the things we do. Many self-development books tell you to surrender your ego and pride completely. For many of us though, our ego is embedded firmly into our identity and it is difficult to separate from it. To surrender your ego takes practice and discipline and if you let it go too soon you might start haemorrhaging and have a total ego relapse.

Ok...maybe not.

Some of us may not even want to let go of our ego. For most of us, we don't want to live in a constant state of guru bliss, at least not yet. We only want for some sense, order, and purpose in our lives.

It is healthy to surrender some of your ego because it can get in the way of achieving what you need to achieve. The element of conformity and trying to please others all the time can cloud your judgements and choices, but there are parts of my ego that I like and will keep around when I choose.

Completely surrendering your ego is wonderfully enlightening. It is rejuvenating to feel a deep quiet state of bliss but I know that to live the mantra and be the change I want to see in the world, I am going to have to enjoy my physical association and my ego.

Our ego can be a positive identity. It can drive us to change and impact the world. I like the feeling of someone loving my work. I like the feeling of achievement and being proud of what I have done and how far I have come. I like being happy and content and a part of that comes from my pride.

I am a Leo. You can't ask a Leo to surrender their ego. That's like asking a pianist to cut off his fingers.

The secret is to ask yourself why you make certain choices and whether or not they are your own choices or those choices were to conform to another's ideals. Your ego is a double-edged sword. You need to identify which elements are serving to help you and which are hindering you and blocking your path.

An example of your ego at play may be how you manage relationships. Are you impulsive? Do you enjoy the thrill of the chase and get bored when you have captured your prey? Do you enjoy being adored? Do you crave affection?

When you are in a relationship, have a look at what you are giving of yourself and offering the other person. You may find the emptiness you feel is a reflection of what is inside yourself and what you are giving or taking.

Ego can be seductive. It has an appetite and is never satisfied for long by material or superficial satisfaction. It wants for more. It has a taste and wants for something bigger or better. It compares itself to everyone else and can devour you if you let it.

Ego itself is not a 'bad' thing. It is only something to fear or avoid if you allow yourself to fall for the seduction and allow yourself to be devoured. As with everything in good measure, it can be good for the soul to indulge in small moments.

Sometimes after a hard day, it can lift your spirits when a loved one tells you that you are beautiful. Sometimes when you are feeling tired or exhausted or burned out, it is fine to indulge in a little bit of a wallow.

Don't let it become a habit, and be conscious of your thoughts for the majority and you will not stray too far.

The ego is what holds grudges. The ego can hold onto negativity that only sabotages you. The ego owns grudges. They come from resentment, a need to be right or have revenge in some form.

I have had trouble freeing myself of feelings of resentment towards people who have hurt me very deeply. I have struggled at times to find the capacity within myself to forgive them and be free of my negativity towards them.

I know that resentment and hate hold me back. I know that it makes me feel bad and I know that the only way to remove that is to forgive. As much as I would like to say that I forgive easily and I often do, there have been times when I just did not have the tools or could not get my mind around a way to really forgive and be free.

Try It!

I would be in no position to ask anyone to consider forgiving others if I could not achieve it myself. This chapter I have struggled with because I know that even up until last week, I still held that resentment, but now I am confident to write this chapter because I have found a way to manage forgiveness and it is working very well.

The challenge is in shifting perspective.

I tried several of my usual tools for 'looking outside-in' and disassociating myself, but they were not working because it was felt so deeply.

When I was visiting my sister and her newborn child, I had a thought. When we are born, we are perfect in every way. Before us lays a world of infinite possibility.

My sweet little nephew is flatulent, spews on me, soils his pants and then smiles.

We forgive a child anything because we know that they have a lifetime of learning and possibility in front of them.

Sometimes we say, 'They don't know any better', and quite often, they don't.

When I think of those people who have wronged me, I now wipe the slate. I consider today the first day of the rest of their life. What is in the past is gone. Their actions come from their own belief system and the values they have been taught. If they continue to repeat those actions that is their lesson to learn but it no longer affects me.

I visualise them as a newborn. They are going to make mistakes and they will repeat their mistakes until they learn. I have removed myself from their path, separated myself, and can now accept them as they are.

The newborn is such a powerful metaphor that it really makes a deep impact and it feels good to finally be free of resentment. We are all here on our own journeys. Make yours a pleasant one.

Forgiving someone does not mean you have to be their best friend. It just means letting go and moving on with your own life without carrying the baggage of their ego with you.

There is no good and bad. The ego likes labels. There is only perception.

Change your perception and free yourself to make you own choices.

Chapter Twelve

The Dog ate my Homework

The Excuses we Make to Ourselves

Chapter Twelve

"He who excuses himself accuses himself."

Gabriel Meurier

Barry considered himself an artist. He was not just any artist. His craft required a skill that he had developed over many years and finely tuned to such a degree that he considered himself an absolute master of his craft.

Barry was a 'Bullshit' artist.

Barry wore the moniker as a badge of honour.

If he were ten minutes early for work, he would spend fifteen minutes in the toilet, just so he would have an excuse to make an excuse.

His passion for crap started at a very young age. The first time he bullshitted someone was his mum and she later became a great subject for honing his craft.

He recalled it as one of his finest moments.

He was seven, and he had been playing cricket inside the house again. As would be expected when a lad plays cricket inside, he smashed his mother's favourite vase.

It was not worth anything but his mum loved it and would go nuts.

His mum was on the balcony hanging the washing on the line so he had to think quickly.

He glanced out the back and saw her coming towards the house. He hid the ball and started running out the front with his bat high in the air. He ran to the front of the house and crouched down on the ground as if he was chasing something.

He saw his mother follow him. She saw that Barry was chasing something, so assumed that it was an accident.

Barry got up and told her that a feral cat was in the house and as he tried to shoo it away, he broke the vase. He threw in a few tears for good measure and his mother hugged him and said she was very proud.

Ever since that sweet victory, Barry practiced his craft on everyone.

He would have three girlfriends at once. He created impressive qualifications and phoney degrees to get high paying jobs which he also managed to fudge his way though.

One would expect that at some point, people would find out, but nobody ever did. He was just that good.

He always came out on top. One day, it all came crashing down around him.

Barry had been having stomach cramps for three months so went to get some tests done, and as he sat in front of his doctor, his world fell apart when he found out that he had a rare terminal disease with a lengthy name.

With just months to live, Barry re-evaluated his life, as terminal patients often do.

What would be his legacy? Why was this happening?

Barry decided to do the biggest deception he had ever done. He decided that because he was so good at bullshitting, he would bullshit the disease.

He stopped making excuses and deceiving everyone else and focused his entire bullshitting arsenal on deceiving his body into believing it was well again.

Morning, noon and night, every day, he deceived his body. He hypnotised himself and he put pictures of athletes up on all the walls.

He read books and went to fitness classes and he did start to feel better.

He was actually convincing himself that there never was any illness.

Two months later, he returned to the doctor and underwent another round of tests.

It had worked. Barry was healthy again. Not all excuses are bad but he decided it might be time for a new craft.

The excuses we often make to ourselves to justify our laziness and our addiction to mediocrity often boil down to three categories.
- Courage
- Time Management
- Finances

You will need to master all three to make significant changes in your life, however once you get past the initial discomfort, with repetition and daily success habits, they will soon become second nature and you'll be on auto-pilot and the momentum and outcomes will amaze you.

When you start seeing the results you can achieve and realise how much control you really do have, you will be inspired and encouraged to keep with it. You will strengthen your resolve and achieve more.

Each of these excuses has an emotional element.

Courage is associated with fear and has the strongest emotional grounding and can therefore produce some difficult blocks to lasting change. Courage can take some time to master first. Sometimes we are not even aware of the fears we have. They are so far embedded into our subconscious that we don't even know they exist.

We covered some of the foundations of fear in chapter six and I will suggest some useful tools in Part three that can help further with identifying and clearing some of these blocks.

Time Management is associated with ego and sometimes we would rather do nothing at all instead of something we dislike, even if the eventual outcome is to our favour.

Sometimes, making the choice to do something and pushing yourself to do the first step can pull you over this block. Repetition also helps with overcoming blocks. If you have achieved something once, you know you can do it repeatedly.

Unfamiliar territory is always daunting at first, but when you have trodden the path, felt the elation and the pride of achievement, and seen the results, it is exhilarating.

De-programming yourself is another solution to the time management excuses we make. Fake it till you make it.

We create our own mind blocks and can therefore unmake them too. The 4-minute mile is a prime example. As soon as that record was broken and the mile was run in less than 4 minutes, that mind barrier was broken and others achieved what was impossible before then.

Finances are always an easy enough excuse but if you change your perspective, they can also be a huge motivator.

It is human to want for security, freedom and choice. Improve your relationship with money and wealth and this last barrier will be nothing more than a minor obstacle.

If you can overcome your excuses, and couple them with an unyielding faith in yourself, you can achieve astounding results. I have learned that regardless of what your faith is, it is the faith and the belief itself that makes things happen.

When you look at someone praying for a loved one and projecting that love and that absolute faith, there is a power and energy in the room. You can feel it.

When you are in a sports ground, watching a marathon with everyone hoping for their guy to win. There is a powerful energy in the stadium.

When a mother can lift a car to save her child, her power comes from an energy she didn't know she had until it was needed. During those moments, love and faith were more important than doubt or excuses. The powerful energy to make things happen comes from passion, love and belief.

Try It!

You can anchor those feelings and use them whenever you want on cue. They can help you be strong when you need that strength.

When I mentioned each of the scenarios in the previous paragraph, those sentences would have evoked an emotion in you because you have seen them before and you have experienced those emotions.

Try this exercise.

When you look back over your own past, think of a time where you were swelling with complete inspiration. Think of a time when the hairs on the back of your neck tingled with excitement, and where you have been inspired with absolute happiness and joy, been lost in the moment, and totally overcome.

As you hold onto that thought, notice the smells that were around you, the colours and the sounds and as you notice the sounds, smells, colours and the feelings within yourself, imagine a knob on your wrist where you can turn it up and magnify it.

Magnify those colours, smells, sounds and feelings. Let yourself experience those feelings and as you do, gently rub the knuckle of your first finger. Stop rubbing your knuckle and slowly let the feelings and that vision fade and let the thought drift away.

You can use it to anchor any emotion to any part of your body and call on those anchors whenever you need them. The more you use them, the more effective they are. You can relive any moment in your life that you choose. Your memory and emotions can be a powerful tool that you have complete control over.

When you need that feeling again, fire off the anchor, (in this case rub the knuckle), and your body responds accordingly.

You have most likely heard of Pavlov's dog.

The term refers to someone who reacts to a situation rather than using the process of critical thinking.

Ivan Pavlov conducted an experiment where he would signal the feeding time for the dog by ringing a bell, and soon found that it was not the food that would cause the dog to salivate, but the ringing of the bell. The dog was 'conditioned' to respond to that anchor.

You can have positive anchors and negative anchors. As you notice your responses to different stimuli, notice how you feel and react, and replace the negative anchors with new positive anchors such as the one we have just created.

This is a good tool for establishing a positive focus and mindset and in turn as you see results, your belief system, faith and trust in what you can achieve will grow.

When you feel doubt beginning to arise or you find yourself making excuses, fire off an anchor and just focus on taking the next step towards your goal.

Chapter Thirteen

Making the Minutes Count

Managing Time and Living a Life that Matters

Chapter Thirteen

"Not everything that counts can be counted and not everything that can be counted counts"

Sign hanging in Einstein's office at Princeton

The Creator's laboratory was an interesting place. There were white fluffy clouds delicately drifting around the lab. Shelves of bibs and bobs and various creations in different states of being were meticulously organised.

Some of her slightly unfinished or not-quite-as-expected experiments lived in little pens around the room, and others ran free-range in the scenic valley outside.

She loved them all dearly and equally and accepted that each was a beauty to behold, even if they were not as she had anticipated.

The Creator was a kind woman and took great pride in her work. She was extremely well organised and planned her days well enough that she had had time to rest on every seventh day without a care of mind or trouble to ponder.

She valued time as one of her greatest triumphs. Time was one of her more abstract creations and it was perfect in its flexibility and openness for interpretation to the perceptions of each who cared to look upon it. Time was like an infinite mood ring. Whether it is perceived as something good or bad was dependant on who was considering it and their frame of reception.

Some days it would shine a brilliance of silver for one man and a choking, muddy brown for yet another in the very same exact moment within time.

Both men have the same allocation and choice of its expenditure, yet they both perceived it with such a vastly different value.

One man would cherish every moment of his time. He would collect memories and relive them in his moments of silence so that he was a rich man in every respect.

Another man would toil, ponder his misgivings, and go home weak, hungry, and feeling the incompleteness of never having enough time.

The Creator sat on her thinking chair admiring her work as she looked down at her creations exploring their worlds within the valley of freedom and opportunity.

Before time, there was no value so she created it as a measure of value. Before 'Something', 'Nothing' did not exist because it had nothing to be measured against.

Time was more valuable than any other creation yet few saw it for the blinding pursuit of all that shines and seduces one away from their true worth.

Every so often, The Creator would send a messenger down to the valley to show the world what a great gift they held, and every so often, someone would listen and they would become rich within their own world of opportunity.

All the messengers she sent carried the same truth and spoke the same message.

'Time cannot be forced or stolen. Time cannot be taken away from you but you can freely give it. It is the most valuable asset you have and the one of which we are all born to in equal measure every day.'

Every messenger carried back news of their outcome and increasingly each saw a change beginning to emerge. Time will soon be seen for all its glory and the creations in the valley would know that what they sought so blindly was in front of their eyes all along.

Chapter Thirteen - Making the Minutes Count

When you look back over the moments throughout your own life, you will notice that the more significant memories are the ones that had an emotional grounding.

Do you know where you were when you heard about Princess Diana's car accident?

Where were you when you heard about September 11?

Time is of no importance if it has no value attached to it.

I know both of those above examples are traumatic and sad ones, but tragic events seem to have a lasting impact on our long term memory and they are both extraordinary in their strength of how they affected people on an individual level and as a united world.

Do you remember how many emails you sent today? Do you remember how many gear changes you made driving home from the store?

Both of those exercises took time, but they did not carry any weight because they were commonplace.

If you life is a series of gear changes, bill payments, emails and 9-5 working days, the monotony of the treadmill can lead to resentment, dissatisfaction and illness.

If you find that you do not seem to have enough hours in your day to get everything done, yet your neighbour seems to spend all his time on holidays and with his kids while still having enough to get by, perhaps you need to place a higher value on your own time.

Do you remember when you were a child how you would 'lose' time? When was the last time you 'lost' time? If you removed stress and anxiety from your life by managing your time more effectively, your mind would be free to get lost now and then.

Managing your time and decreasing stress in your life actually results in greater opportunities for spontaneity as it allows you to be conscious of your priorities and 'free' to make sound judgements and choices within your own personal rulebook and boundaries.

When did you stop giving yourself playtime? When did you stop losing yourself in the moment? When did you start to feel obliged to do things that you did not enjoy? Why do you do things you do not enjoy?

Have you ever had one of those days where you are run off your feet all day but you get to the end of the day and have nothing to show for it? You've got ten million things to do, so you do a bit of each then get distracted and chase after something else before going off on another tangent and before you know it, another day has passed and you're no closer to getting anything completed.

Mothers are notorious for it. Everyone places demands on you - your spouse, your kids, your boss, yourself.

STOP. Breathe. Relax.

If you plan your time and you are aware of your priorities, you will not feel stress. If you spend your days, hours and minutes doing only that which is important to you, your days start to mean something. You start to achieve things and everything seems to fall into place.

By taking the time out to organise your day, you will save time in the overall schematic of your daily activities.

Many people do not plan and make the excuse, 'I don't have time to plan, and I'm too busy.'

15 minutes out of your day planning the next day's activities can save you hours of time chasing your tail.

Look at where you presently spend your time. Think about your week and how much time you would spend on these activities:

- Watching TV
- Reading the newspaper
- Social media,
- Surfing the net and chatting online with friends

All of those activities are fun activities. I am not going to tell you to stop them entirely. We need our down time. However, you would likely do at least one or all three of those activities in a day.

Allocate a specific allotment of time to those activities each day and spend no more than that allotment of time. Be firm and disciplined with yourself.

From the time you have previously spent on those activities, allocate yourself just 15 minutes every evening or in the morning if you prefer and that time is for planning your daily schedule and nothing else.

Planning your time, as with planning anything, results in reduced stress, predictive outcomes and successful rituals and habits.

Start to value your time.

When you value your time, you will be a lot choosier on how you spend it. We spend more time choosing how we will spend our money than how we spend our time.

Our time is the most valuable asset we have. Once it has gone, you cannot get it back.

With money, you can spend it and then make more. With time, you spend it and it is gone. It is forever lost to the passages of time.

Think about it. Think about the most precious moments in your life. Think about cuddles with your mum when you were a kid. Think about cuddling your own children or laughing with friends. Think about how they made you feel. Notice yourself smiling and cherish those moments.

How long did each of those moments last? They were most likely not very long at all. Most of them would be ten to fifteen minutes. Nobody can take them from you. They are yours to keep, but when you think of the value of those moments, be conscious of how you spend your time now. What can you do in 15 minutes that will affect you for the rest of your life?

What can you do in the next fifteen minutes to make another person's life happier? We all have the same amount of hours in a day. It all boils down to how you choose to spend them.

Chances are you're wasting your precious time on some activities and they are not making your life any richer. Think of the time you spend on those activities and people and think where you could better spend that time.

Try It!

The first step in effective time management is to evaluate your priorities. If you had more time, what would you ideally like to be doing with it?

If you won 30 million dollars tomorrow and never had to work again for the rest of your life, what would you spend your time doing?

Write it down. It is a fun exercise. Firstly visualise yourself looking at your bank account statement with the balance of $30 002 078.45.

I made it an odd number so that it was more believable. It works more effectively if you take a bit of time and create a document on your computer that looks like a bank statement, but visualising will work too.

Imagine yourself with the surety that the cheque will clear, and it is in your account and all you have to do now is decide what you are going to do with it. Don't worry about the feelings of 'I didn't earn it', or the criticisms of others for now. Just imagine it is there.

What would you do, if you had that amount in your bank account?

What is important to you?

Would you spend more time with your family?

Would you travel?

Would you buy your own business and have someone run it for you?

Would you go to university and study something you always wanted to?

Would you get your pilots license and buy a plane?

Would you buy a new house?

Would you buy all your family a new house?

With whom would you share it?

Would you spend more time on charity work or donate some of the money?

What did you enjoy doing as a child?

As you go through the list, you will get more and more ideas. Write them down and soon a theme will start to appear.
Now write down where you presently spend most of your time. If it is at work, what parts of the work take up the most time? When you are at home, what do you spend most of your time doing?
You will soon see the contrast in your priorities, desired values, and the way you currently spend your time.
Create a small list of your personal values. These will be broader conceptual 'trademarks' that you can use as a guidebook to live by. They will identify you.
My own personal values are three statements:

'Don't just take what each day brings. Bring something to each day.'

This one deals specifically with time management. It is very important to me and helps me create moments of value and achieve my outcomes. If I find myself being distracted or procrastinating, I guide myself back to this value and identify with it.

My second personal value statement is:

'Be the change you want to see in the world.' (Ghandi)

I use this for my goal setting and life purpose. If I find something upsets me, or a problem arises, I seek to find the solution.

My third mantra is the Golden Rule:

'I aspire to be the sort of person I would want as a friend.'

This is how I manage my relationships and communication with other people. It's a twist on the law of reciprocity, karma, and the 'Do unto others' commandment.

Be creative when you come up with your personal value statements.

Think about what you would like people to say about you when you pass away. Writing your own eulogy is a great way to get some ideas for your personal values.

Do a 'Google' search for visionary statements and life principles and rewrite them in your own words. Make them entertaining or assign some value. Don't have too many, as they will be too hard to remember. Between one and five is a good number.

Once you have established your own personal values, you can use these as a guide for how to manage your time on a day-to-day basis.

The next step is to plan your daily activities.

Buy a diary and every day, start the day in a mindset of gratitude. When you rise in the morning, consciously think to yourself 'Thank you for this day. This day is a gift. That's why it's called the present.'

This part of your planning schedule will not take long and is a very effective tool when it comes to planning your day. Think about what you are grateful for in your life. It could be your family, your house, your car, and your friends. Whatever it is, write it down in your diary. These are good notes to come back to when you feel your mind wandering into negativity or stress.

Always remember that you have a fresh new day. Everything from yesterday is in the past. Not everything in the future is determined yet.

Think of any problems you have and only challenge the ones that you can fix today. Put the rest on the mental ice shelf and let it drift away. It doesn't matter to you today if you can't fix it, manage it, or deal with it today. The day will come when you are ready to manage that problem, but if today is not that day, spare it no further thought.

Prioritise your tasks according to your higher priorities and value system.

Create lists in order of priority and if something doesn't get done, don't stress it. It was not meant to be and its time will come. Have just three main tasks you need to do each day and keep the rest flexible or on a master list where you can choose to do them later when you have the time available.

Look at your to-do list for today.

Pay attention to which tasks you want to do, and which tasks you do not want to do.

Can they be outsourced?

Are they your own priorities or someone else's? (If they are someone else's priorities; is that someone else an adult? Give it back to them. If it is not yours, let it go.)

At the end of each day, take your diary out and write down what you have achieved for that day. Write down what you have had control over today and how you are feeling. Plan some activities and priorities for the following day and always make sure that they are your own and in line with your own values.

Let your values define you and your choices and you will soon find yourself with plenty of 'spare' time and a lot more personal satisfaction.

As you go through further chapters, you will discover exactly what your time is worth. When you live by your values, you will soon realise many of the tasks you do in a day could be outsourced. This can be done cost effectively to free up some of your own personal time.

A note on outsourcing - Sometimes we try to do everything ourselves. Just because you can do something, doesn't mean you should do it.

When you renovate a house, don't try to do the whole lot yourself. Your time is better spent on other activities. You need to value your time and know what your time is worth. Identify what tasks can be outsourced and leverage your time and skills to their best advantage.

You don't need to outsource locally. There are a few websites where you can outsource anything from having a virtual personal assistant, to copywriting, to web design. Any administrative task you can think of; you can outsource.

I use a website called 'oDesk'. What these sites do is create a portal between someone who wants a service and a freelance professional. There are professionals on these sites from all over the world.

To use them, you create an advertisement with what your project or task entails and your budget, and the database places the advertisement. Freelance professionals submit their best 'bid' and application.

A service that may cost you $1000 locally may only cost you $2 an hour internationally and the level of service will be highly comparable.

The beauty of electronic media is that you can load your advert, read through the applications, find your employee, and go to bed. The project will be in your inbox by the morning.

When you plan your daily activities, think ahead on the tasks you can outsource and decide to write an advertisement instead of doing everything yourself.

Chapter Fourteen

Oh my! What Pretty Gold Teeth you have!

How to make Sound Financial Judgements

Chapter Fourteen

"But wait...There's more!"

Tim Shaw

'Can I have a volunteer from the audience?'

A feeble hand went up. A frail girl stumbled forward. She was dressed in rags and leant upon a stick.

'My dear girl, could you tell me what ails ya?'

The odd-looking man helped the young waif onto the back of his wagon.

'Well Suh, me Ma passed away just last spring when a wagon fell on her. I tried to save her Suh, but the wagon fell on me leg and I canna walk no more. I had such pretty things, but now I sell buttons for me bread. I could be a great dancer if only I could walk.'

'Well my dear girl, my Elixir will cure that leg of yours.'

'Really Suh? That is too kind.' She said humbly.

The frail girl shed a tear as the man offered her a swig from the dirty bottle in his hand. The crowd watched on expectantly at the well-rehearsed performance.
The label on the bottle read 'Guru Maharaaji's Rare Snake Elixir'. It had a picture of a man wearing a turban and some eastern looking clothes. He had grey hair and was clearly of European origin but the label told a woeful tale of his parents being killed in the Orient where he was raised by Wisemen in the old ways of the east. He had now brought back the secrets in the form of a rare and exotic snake oil that would cure any ailment.

The crowd gathered closer. They had to have some of the snake oil. The Guru only had a limited supply and would not be going back to the East for another six months.

Women swapped their valuables for the elixir and the promise of restored youth. Men gave gold purses and their watches and finery to purchase as many bottles as they could. It was a fine investment and when the original supply ran out; their elixirs would be worth ten times more than their purchase value.

When the guru moved on to the next town with his magical snake elixir, the wake of his presence remained. For some of the townsfolk, the elixir actually worked, even though it was nothing more than watered down rum and castor oil. The value of their perception and belief had made it worth more than any substance.

Some of the men on-sold theirs and turned a small profit. Some men held onto their investments for want of a higher return.

Some of the women indulgently took their elixir every day in the hope of youthful promises. The elixir was the talk of the town. Women fought over it. Pickpockets stole it and sold it in the back alleys of town to the highest bidder. A black market formed and it grew in value.

One day, a young lad who worked in the local pharmacy saw the value in the famed elixir. He sold his bicycle to buy a bottle and set about finding the secret formula, hoping that he could somehow duplicate its mystical powers. It did not take him long to discover the true ingredients of the famed cure-all and he promptly told the authorities.

The salesman was long gone by then but laws were now in place and anyone found selling the elixir would be charged as a scoundrel.

Friends turned on friends who had sold them their last quantities. The lower class women who could not afford the elixir scoffed at the fine ladies who had coveted it so passionately. Men tried to re-brand their elixirs as other miracle cures, just to regain their losses. Fortunes were made and lost over the miracle cure. Nobody wanted to take responsibility for their own stupidity.

A town meeting was called where the townsfolk could find a way to recover from the financial devastation the elixir had caused. The townsfolk, fresh from their loss, agreed that they needed to protect themselves from such manipulation.

A decree was nailed at the town's entrance:

'All salesmen must have a license to operate - This license can be bought at the Mayor's office.'

Chapter Fourteen - Oh my, What Pretty Gold Teeth you Have!

'All medicinal products have to undergo a rigorous bout of testing before being approved for sale - This testing can be done for a fee at the Mayor's office.'

'Everyone has to consult a licensed moneychanger before making any purchase over a specified amount - Anyone wanting to be a moneychanger can buy their license at the Mayor's office.'

They came up with more and more rules, and the Mayor became rather wealthy with all the new licenses he was issuing.

As some of the wealthier townsfolk started to see that they had surrendered their ownership and responsibility, one by one, they bought their own licenses to operate freely as they did before the salesman's deception and they started using their new licenses to act on behalf of others - still untrained and no wiser than before.

Those without licenses handed over their money to those who had them thinking they had a hidden wisdom, and lo behold, the snake oil was back in circulation.

Have you ever done anything a bit risky and felt the thrill of nearly being caught? I always catch myself with a devious smile on my face just thinking about my own misadventures.

We all like to live a little dangerously now and then. It gets your heart pumping, and that rush of challenging authority is racy. It makes you know you're alive.

Adrenalin junkies live on that rush. The moment of doing something dangerous where you can't control the outcome is addictive.

It is good for the soul to let loose a little bit. However, at some point we need to take responsibility for being irresponsible.

Everything has its limits and sometimes we are caught. What's the first thing most people do when they are caught? Point the finger or look for someone to blame.

Many of us don't grow out of this pattern and it permeates into every facet of our lives.

People sue each other for their own stupidity. You hear stories about a man getting drunk and jumping in front of a car then suing the owner of the pub and the driver of the car.

People complain to the government if they lose money in shares or are conned. They read the article on how to get rich, they make the choice to invest their money into it, but when it goes bankrupt, they don't want to take responsibility for their actions.

Finance and investment has an element of risk. Educate yourself thoroughly and minimise those risks.

Because of the diminishing capacity for our population to take responsibility for their own actions, we have financial planners whose sole purpose now is to sell financial products where they can offset their liability.

We have talented and highly skilled surgeons who decide to become general practitioners instead because they're afraid of the liability and risk of making split second decisions when they attempt to save a life.

You need to make a choice and take ownership of every decision and choice you have made. You can say you made a decision under duress. You can say that you were intimidated. You can say you were misrepresented, but when push comes to shove, *You* still made that decision.

In my own recent experience, I found that a finance company told me a fable resulting in the classic caveat emptor *'Buyer Beware'*.

I'm aware of my 'rights' and the legalities of the credit code, but ultimately, I accept responsibility for believing and trusting the salesperson and not reading the fine print. We all have to take responsibility for our stupidity.

I have to take responsibility for my choices and actions and take measurable steps to alleviating the fallout from those choices. Have a look at your own life. Think about where you might be laying the blame on others.

Remember the rose metaphor from Chapter Two.

They are just behaving and reacting to life with the tools and resources they have. Accept this. Accept others as they are and accept responsibility for your own actions. Control your own outcomes and lead by example.

In finance when you own your outcomes, the effort will reward you.

Sometimes that reward is in the form of a lesson that needs to be learned. Recognise the lesson, and move on towards a better future.

You've seen those advertisements and had a call from the telemarketer asking if you want to attend a free seminar where you can find out how to own ten properties in 3 weeks. It's easy - no money down. You'll save copious amounts of tax and receive a passive income of 80% *(with a disclaimer in fine print saying – 'refer to–clause XYZ section 2b').*

When I owned my real estate agency, I decided to do my Diploma of Financial Planning. My intention was to educate myself and offer an additional service to my clients as most of them were looking at ways to manage their investments and savings.

What I learned when I did this course was that Financial Planning is a license to *sell* financial products. It entails very little in the way of actual financial advice. One of the first lessons you will learn as an aspiring financial planner is how to assess your client's needs and align them with a financial product that will give them a safe, low return.

In Australia, there is an act called 'The Financial Services Reform Act'. The act is supposed to protect the consumer. As a result, few financial planners give you any advice on how to best manage your risk or determine the outcomes of your own returns. They will instead, learn what products they can sell you that will shift liability from themselves and onto the company of the product they are selling. They are afraid to give you advice because you could spin around and sue them.

In order to protect people from their own lack of judgment and responsibility, the reform act has made it difficult to find a financial planner who will advise you on high return/high risk products such as derivatives, CFD's or futures. Contracts for Difference were not even covered it the course I took.

The act has removed your choice to decide how much risk you want to take when you are seeking advice. There are still some good planners out there but you do need to shop around. Anyone can become a financial planner regardless of how much experience they have had managing their own investments; that is of course making the broad assumption that they actually have any investments at all. To become a financial planner, all you need to do is complete the course and apply for the license.

Fortunately there is a light at the end of the tunnel. You can take responsibility for your own finances and seek to learn more about investing yourself. We live in an age where there is more information available than ever before.

At first the language can be a bit intimidating and confusing but as with anything, as you continue to seek further learning experiences, you will become familiar with the industry and will soon be knowledgeable on every facet of your investment.

Before you consider investing though, you will need to assess a few things. The first and most important factor in financial management is a consistent budget. I have outlined a basic budget at the end of this chapter.

The next step is to consider the 'structure' of your investment. Leave this one to the professionals. Hire a solicitor and an accountant and get recommendations on the best structure to suit your needs.

There are many structures to consider, Trading names, Intellectual Property Licensing, Propriety Limited Companies, Family Trusts, and Discretionary trusts. Each comes with their own costs, risks and benefits. If asset protection is more important to you than tax savings, one will come out over another as a preferred structure.

If you are a high-income earner and your partner is a low-income earner, your structure can be worked to the most avantageous way for this position. With structuring your finances, one size doesn't fit all.

Your industry may have many tax-deductible items. You may be able to claim depreciation on your investments, property, fixtures or improvements.

Getting advice from specialists for the most appropriate legal and accounting structure will be the best investment you make. If you make the wrong decisions here by going the 'do it yourself' route, it may end up costing you a lot more in the long term.

When you are ready to start investing, you will need to consider the type of investing you wish to do.

There are three main investment vehicles. They are:

- Business
- Stock markets
- Property

I will only touch on each and give an overview only. At the end of the book, there is a reference section for recommended reading and further study.

Business

You can invest several ways in a business directly. You can be a small business owner, a franchisee, self employed, a silent partner, a venture capitalist.

When deciding on whether or not owning a business is for you. You will need to educate yourself and decide whether or not you wish to work in that business or if you will have others managing the day-to-day operations for you. Owning a business can deliver a steady income stream, but it can also break you if you do not educate yourself on what to look for and how to manage it. A solid business uses systems, processes and a business plan with marketing, budgeting and contingency planning in place.

When it comes to business, if you fail to plan, you plan to fail.

Stock Market and Derivatives

Various stories abound on where the first stock market emerged. Uncle Jerry swears the Dutch started it, others say it was the Romans and others say it started in a café in England.

Regardless of its origins, the stock markets of the world are a great way to get your teeth into owning a piece of a business without having to manage it or be a CEO. The internet has made the world a much smaller place and you can now trade on any stock market in the world. When you throw currency trading in the mix, you can boost any profits made and trade around the clock.

Beyond stock trading, there are other products; abstract investments derived from stock trends. These are 'Derivatives'. Some derivatives are Futures, Contracts for Difference, Options and Warrants.

For every stock or product there's probably ten million different ways to invest or trade with them.

When it comes to stocks and derivatives, you need to identify your purpose and know yourself and your reasons for trading or investing. You need to identify yourself as either a *'trader'* or an *'investor'*.

A *'trader'* seeks short-term capital gains and trades on the day-to-day price fluctuations of a stock.

An *'investor'* will seek to hold the asset and will invest for income streams from dividends or long-term capital gains.

Both investors and traders have their own ways of planning their returns and managing their assets. When you determine which class you want to be a part of, you can then learn only the information specific to that methodology and avoid confusing yourself.

Stock and derivative trading can be an exciting way to make money, but you will find with most investment vehicles, the balance of the risk to reward ratio is relative. The higher the potential returns, the higher the risk.

There are ways to minimise risk and add stops and limits to your orders, but as with anything, educating yourself is the best way to manage and reduce your risk.

How long will it take you to learn everything about stock trading? How long is a piece of string? Most people start 'paper trading' first. This is a good safe way to cut your teeth. It involves picking trades, following the market 'on paper' or 'in theory', and testing your plan.

It is a good way to learn systems to find one to suit you, however only trading live will show you the holes in your trade plan. Have a trade plan, follow it, and only tweak it when necessary. Trading and Stock investments require discipline. If you have no discipline and are a bit edgy, I would suggest staying away from stocks and putting your money in a more low risk investment. Know thine self and take responsibility for your outcomes.

Property

Property is one of the oldest forms of investing. Many property and wealth investors and educators speculate that property prices double on average every seven years.

In 1860, French economist Clement Juglar identified the presence of economic cycles that were usually 7-12 years in duration. Economists base theories and predict outcomes using various forms of the economic cycle. The basic gist of it is that investments, business, economies and property moves in cycles with peaks and troughs and they are all relative to each other. When one sector is performing strongly, another will perform poorly and the cycle continues.

Consistent trends have shown the cycle to be true within the bounds of small deviations. When investing in property. You will once again need to have a level or self-awareness on what your intentions and expected outcomes will be.

There are several reasons people invest in property.

In Australia, there are some tax advantages in gearing your property a certain way to save on tax if you are a high-income earner. This is called 'negative gearing'.

Some people prefer a passive income stream. There are still plenty of cash flow properties available if you look in the right places.

Others like to invest for short term capital gains.

Within property, you can also use some creative finance techniques. These are quite detailed strategies so I will only outline them here and your solicitor will be able to elaborate further on the intricacies of each when you are planning your investments.

For deposits, developers often use insurance bonds and can purchase property with no cash down. When purchasing, 'flipping' or processing a development application, some buyers use options. Options are more often associated with the stock market. They mean a buyer can pay a non-refundable premium for the 'option' but not the obligation to purchase a property at an agreed price at a date in the future.

A 'put' option gives you the right to sell the property and a 'call' option is the right to buy. If you have a put and call option on a property, it can pass through your hands and you can make the difference on the increase in the price without having handed over a single cent.

You will still need to pay stamp duty and capital gains tax from the proceeds as the property does still pass through your hands if you exercise an option, but it is a method of making some quick capital in the right market conditions.

Often developers will do this in a hot market. They will place options on a large piece of land, organise the division and approvals and on sell at a premium with the approvals in place.

Some other creative financing options including venture capital and peer-to-peer finance are starting to become another popular option for short term financing. Make sure you do your homework first.

There are plenty of valuable tools for investing in property.

If you are looking to invest in property and require a synopsis on recent comparable sales in your area, you can access this information from one of several resources and it can help you in doing your research when investing in property.

There are two major providers of this information in Australia, those being RP Data and Property Data Solutions (PDS Live).

When you purchase a home, you details are submitted to the local titles office. They are stored on the database for the Department of Natural Resources register. They in turn allow PDS Live and RP Data to use this information for allowing real estate professionals and consumers to research the property information when making either a purchase or a sale.

Both PDS and RP data also have other features that are highly beneficial including local area snapshots, recent sales, and current listings, any easements on the property, previous sales history, zoning and photos.

It is illegal to use this information for direct marketing or any purpose other than that which it was intended, but it is an effective research tool for determining the current market value property and a great negotiation tool.

Some factors to consider that affect the price of property are:

Locality –
Being close to transport, schools, shopping, water or other amenities is an excellent selling point. If you have a beautiful home next door to the local abattoir …this is not quite so appealing to the wider population.

Condition of the home –
If the home is well presented and in overall good condition with no structural concerns, this will appeal to a wider base of buyers who want to move into a home that does not need any repairs. These buyers are usually owner-occupiers and will more often pay a higher price as it is more of a 'heart' decision. If the house is a 'renovator' and needs work it will appeal to a lower demographic and be a negotiation tool for the buyer.

Current state of the market –
Market conditions are either a *'sellers' market'* or a *'buyers'* market.

In a 'hot' market or a 'sellers' market', the economy is performing well, interest rates are reasonable and unemployment is low. Economic conditions are overall very comfortable and the demand for property exceeds the supply so prices move very quickly and a property boom results. Anyone who sells their home in this type of market will usually achieve a quick sale and a good price as there will be more buyers competing for the property and as such will offer top dollar.

In a 'slow' market or a 'buyers' market', the economy is slow, interest rates are high, unemployment is on the rise and economic conditions are a bit sketchy. A slow market usually occurs after a change of government or a series of significant market movements in other economic environments such as the local stock market or international economic conditions.

In these markets, buyers are more aware, and have less money to spend. This is the best time to buy, as there is usually a 'glut' of property on the market and many people affected by the economy are very eager to sell and are subsequently highly negotiable. Warren Buffet used this psychology on the stock market and buys when these conditions come about and stocks are under-priced.

If you are in a good financial status it is the ideal time to buy, but if you want to sell in this market, expect your buyers to be cautious and a bit tighter on negotiations as they have plentiful stock from which to choose.

Many small investors only focus on the residential market. Do you homework and consider developing, sub divisions, commercial property and other strategies outside the norm.

Take responsibility for your own finances and be in charge of your own wealth.

Try It!

If there is more than one person involved in your financial decisions, you will need to take equal responsibility for the outcomes of any financial management. The biggest reason for most marriage break-ups is money.

Start with a basic budget.

Budgeting does not need to be complicated. Find out what it costs you to live each week and try the 'bucket system'.

The 'Bucket System' goes back centuries.

You have 4 buckets. One is for your living expenses, the next is for your fun and recreation allocation, the next is for your savings, and the last is for your investments.

Use four bank accounts and divvy up between them.

Start by calculating your rent/mortgage, electricity, grocery bill, phone, car and insurance expenses. – work it out into a weekly budget.

From each pay packet, allocate 10% to the recreation budget, 10% to savings, and 10% to investments.

You can change the percentages around as you progress, but it is a good foundation to build your basic budget on.

With any leftover, use it to clear your debts a little bite at a time.

Once you have established your budget, you will need to figure out what sort of investor you are.
If one of you is high risk, and the other is low risk, spread your investments out over different investment types. Perhaps one of you can take responsibility for the 'high risk' and the other can manage the 'low risk'.

Some questions to ask yourself:

How much time do you want to spend on managing your investments?

How much do you want to learn?

What sort of returns do you want?

Do you want cash flow (an ongoing income stream) or capital (a bulk amount from the sale or growth of an asset)?

Why do you want to invest?

Are you nearing retirement?

Are you interested in tax savings?

Is there anyone else involved in your financial decisions?

What is your aversion to risk? How much are you prepared to risk getting your returns?

Review your investments regularly and remember to reward yourself.

Chapter Fifteen

The Love Boat

Is it Love or do you have your Beer Goggles on?

Chapter Fifteen

"Love doesn't make the world go round. Love is what makes the ride worthwhile"

Franklin P. Jones

The Universe was hosting a great ball. It had been anticipated by all who were attending but nobody knew what was about to happen. The greatest love of all time was to unfold before them and from it would spring such wonders as had never been seen before.

Earth was young. She wore a sheer gown of the most delicate blue and within it you could see flecks of every colour. She radiated a youthful innocence that caught the eye of Sun as he watched her gliding past. It was at this moment, when he first saw Earth, that he fell in love with her.

Many planets tried to catch Sun's eye at the great ball but Sun could not see past the radiant Earth. Sun asked Earth if she would grace him with a dance. She looked up towards him and loved him too. Together they danced; never taking their eyes from one another.

Sun shone more brightly and warmth radiated from him as he glowed and the love grew for his beloved Earth. Together they danced across the Universe until they fell into a melodic rhythm. He spun his beloved around him. Other planets joined the dance and watched on and enjoyed the warmth of Sun's love radiating.

Sun and Earth never stopped their dance. Earth felt safe in the warmth and strength of her loving Sun. Sun gained his own strength from the adoring gaze of his delicate Earth. They brought each other balance and harmony.

They laughed together and cried together. When Earth shed a tear, Sun would shine brighter to dry her tears and they never stopped their dance. Earth spun around Sun and he held her in his watchful and protective gaze and promised to love her for as long as love could exist.

They had a child and named her Dawn. Dawn soon had a sister and they named her Time.

Dawn and Time grew in the glow of their parent's love and hoped one day to experience a similar love themselves. Dawn found her own love in Dusk and Time found her like soul in Space.

Sun and Earth continued to dance. They looked down at their beautiful children and Sun glowed brighter and Earth was more radiant. Their children had children of their own.

Dawn and Dusk gave birth to twins and named them Night and Day.

Time and Space had a son and named him Infinity.

Sun and Earth continued to dance. They grew older in each other's loving embrace as each generation gave birth to another and each experienced their own love and raised their own family.

Generation after generation they smiled down on their many children and whenever their children were lost, Sun and Earth would guide their children home.

They knew the love that existed within each of their children for every generation was born from the greatest love that ever existed. They would always be safe when they found that little piece of Sun and Earth within themselves.

Chapter Fifteen - The Love Boat

Love - The one word that has inspired the passion, envy, hurt and exhilaration of poets, lovers, politicians, artists and an eternity of tears both joyful and of sorrow.

What is love?

Is love a feeling or a state of being?

Is love an emotion?

What is it to be in-love?

We all have differing opinions on what love is and whether it exists at all. Everyone has the measure of their own life experiences to look back on and swim in.

Love can inspire and make you feel invincible and blind to any ills around you. Love can be painful and sink your heart to despair. I don't know what love is for you. I don't think love is measured by how someone makes you feel. I think love is measured by how much you want to give.

Love is limitless. It has no bounds. By allowing another person in your life, it doesn't displace someone who was already there. There is always room to love another.

The two great loves I have experienced are:

A parent's love is a gift so precious that to lose it would be a vast chasm of emptiness. When you have a child and you sniff their head and it swells up inside you– that is the love of parenthood. You breathe in the essence of that child and want to make their world perfect so they will never feel pain. You kiss their tender forehead and lose time as you sit and watch each breath they take – a parent's love is such a wonderful gift to hold in your heart.

When your child presses every button on the lift and you endure the scathing looks of the other occupants but still find it in your heart to smile – that is a love only a parent can understand.

A lover's love - When a lover wraps you in their arms and you feel safe and trust them with your whole being – such is the joy of a lover. Your skin quivers at the touch of theirs, your lips sink into those of your lover and for a brief moment you become one. You gaze into the eyes of your loved one as they take their last breath and your heart breaks because you cannot go with them – love is painful but so wonderful at the same time.
When you see their flaws and love them for those flaws. When you accept them as they are and want to bring peace into their world – you are in love. Time has no place in the moments you collect together, and you cast all judgements aside and you commit to evolving and growing together and show each other acts of kindness – that is the love of a lover.

Lovers may come and go. Some may be brief. Some may last a lifetime. You may live the fairy tale or you may be a tragic romantic and wear your heart on your sleeve. Perhaps, you may be waiting for the right one – your prince charming or fairytale princess… wait and be willing to surrender to it when it comes.

If you have had a broken heart in the past, let it go. It doesn't serve you to hold past regret and judge others by your experiences. Cast judgements aside. Don't rush it or force love into your schedule. Let it breathe like a fine glass of wine and let it evolve and grow.

Be true to yourself and don't forget to love yourself. Don't be so quick to define your experiences. Let it be and love will touch your heart when you least expect it.

Sometimes love fades. It doesn't mean it never was. It only means it no longer is. Sometimes as people grow and evolve in different directions, the love drifts away.

Your lifetime is your journey. It is a beautiful gift and to share it with another is a wonderful experience but it is also a wonderful experience to capture the joys and laughs in your own time also.

Don't let yourself be so captivated with the ideal of what should be that you lose track of who you are. Lovers should strengthen each other, not place demands on each other or resent each other. Lovers should never lose their own identity or sacrifice who they are to please another. Lovers should grow together but still keep their own spirit alive.

Love can be intoxicating, and it is easy to surrender to the pleasures it can bring. It is beautiful to escape into those beautiful moments where you are lost of all thought outside of your moments.

Chapter Fifteen - The Love Boat

These moments pass though. If you have a deep respect for your lover, you will strengthen each other and carry each other through times of hurt and challenge.

Accept yourself as you are. There are no right or wrong choices. Remember all your choices have been the best ones for you at the time you made them. Focus on the positives. Let the negatives drift away and leave your heart open to the possibilities of new love, whether that is the love of a child, a lover, a friend, a sibling, a parent or a lost puppy.

To build something of value and something that is special requires effort and it doesn't matter whom you are with, when the dust settles and the initial infatuation fades, there needs to be a commitment and a respect to build upon. True love comes from respect, tolerance, kindness and acceptance and its expression is affection, kisses, cuddles and support.

It is important to maintain your own identity but you do also need to surrender a little. If we hold too tightly to 'self' and don't want to give, we will never be able to look into another's eyes and see how beautiful the depths of love can be.

I believe everything in life happens for a reason and everyone comes into your life at a time when you need to learn something about yourself.

When I craved affection, the warmth of a hug and the tenderness of a kiss were enough to fill a void within me that had been lacking for so long. I soon found however, that empty kisses and cold affection bring with them a void and confusion of their own.

Sometimes when life takes a direction you don't understand, you will look at yourself and doubt yourself and wonder what might be so abhorrent that you only seem to attract such emptiness in your life.

When we attract this into our lives, it is because of our lack of self worth on the inside. Fix yourself first. Learn to love yourself and don't dwell on what's lacking. Focus on the beauty of being you and the rest will happen in its own time. To have a heart filled with love is a beautiful gift.

When I started writing this chapter, I thought to myself, 'Who am I to be offering any advice on love?' I've had a failed marriage (I prefer to call it a successful separation) and I'm not exactly the most socially adept person you'll ever meet. I've always been a nerd and a loner, but I still believe that true love exists and one day I will meet a like soul.

I can only speak of my own life experience and what I've learned.

Try It!

After my latest failed attempt at love, I looked across my bedroom at the painting of Jane Avril on my wall and sought her worldly advice. She didn't say anything back. She just flicked her skirt up as the men looked on admirably.

Jane Avril was a famous dancer of the Moulin Rouge and rumoured to be a prostitute. Toulouse Lautrec is one of my favourite artists and he is considered by many to be the father of modern print advertising.

As I stood in front of the giant prostitute advertisement on my bedroom wall, it occurred to me that I have either to start charging for my services, or possibly change the visual stimuli. I couldn't bear to part with the painting so she was moved downstairs.

I created three small pieces for the walls of my room instead. As they are the first image I see every day, they are a very active part of my environment.

Unless you have been living under a rock, you have no doubt heard about 'The Laws of Attraction'. It will not do you any harm to give this a go so open your mind for a moment and work with me here. To have anything of value on the outside, you need to make sure the inside is cared for.

The Laws of Attraction are 'Desire' coupled with an emotional base in action.

It all goes back to mindset as discussed earlier. The first thing to do is decide what you want and why you want it.

Scan over your environment and ask yourself, 'What is your environment projecting?' Change the pictures on your walls and have your environment resonate what you desire.

Change your perception of yourself. If you lack confidence, make a habit of telling yourself every day that you are beautiful in every way.

It might feel a bit awkward at first so just pretend you are someone who is confident as you say it to yourself. If you know of someone who projects the qualities you desire, pretend you are an actor playing the role of that person. Project their personality, then look at yourself in the mirror, and affirm that you are confident and secure and any other qualities you want to instil.

Have a go and try it. Nobody is watching and chances are it just might work.

The following three images are the ones I created for my own wall. You can copy these or create your own. Hanging your own artwork and pieces or vision boards on the wall has a personal touch and carries with it a greater power and ownership.

Figure 15.1 - Love

Figure 15.2 - Family

Figure 15.3 - Respect

Figure 15.4 - Passion

Chapter Sixteen

Betting on the Horse with the Coolest Name

Planning for Life Changing Experiences

Chapter Sixteen

"If I touch a burning candle, I can feel no pain.
If you cut me with a knife, it's still the same.
And I know her heart is beating,
and I know that I am dead;
yet the pain here that I feel,
try and tell me it's not real,
and it seems that I still have a tear to shed."

Corpse Bride – Film by Tim Burton

Dominic was snooping in his grandfather's shed. It was one of his favourite pastimes. Grandad had a knack for collecting all sorts of interesting junk. There was always an adventure in Grandad's shed.

Elijah waited patiently. He was sitting up in Grandad's 1927 Rugby tooting the horn. He loved the old car.

'Aooogah, Aooogah' The horn sounded like someone was strangling a goose. The kids had named the old car 'Ooah' after the noise of the horn.

Elijah was usually content to let Dom do all the ratting around. He would just follow along when he found something interesting.

Dommy kept prodding and exploring. He loved the old trunk on the back of the old car. He had been poking around, when the bottom of the trunk suddenly fell out.

He looked around to make sure Grandad wasn't nearby. He could usually get away with anything with Grandad but he knew that Ooah was Grandad's treasure, and nothing would break Dominic's heart more than to upset Grandad.

He quickly tried to fix the bottom of the trunk. As he was trying to put it back on, he noticed that there were some clips and a secret compartment at the bottom of the trunk. He couldn't help himself; the natural curiosity of a four-year-old boy was more powerful than the wrath of his best friend.

Dominic unclipped the secret compartment and a small leather journal fell out.

He clipped the compartment shut, replaced the bottom of the trunk, and took the journal inside.

Elijah followed, curiously chattering to himself along the way.

Dominic couldn't read, and he knew Grandad would be happy at finding the treasure, so he took the journal inside.

'What's this?' Grandad said as Dominic handed him the journal.

Dom told Grandad where he found it. Grandad went and had a look at the trunk first to see if there was anything else in it, and then he went back inside to examine the journal more closely.

As he opened the journal, an old, worn, carefully folded piece of parchment fell out.

Grandad opened it up, and it was a map. Strangely enough, even though the map appeared to be quite ancient, it was an exact map of his street, it even had houses and small pictures of half complete houses where there was construction going on down the street.

Grandad read the journal. It was the journal of Wilfred Snarpfurth. Wilfred had been a great explorer in his youth. In his journal, he spoke of how his own Grandad gave him the map when he was a boy.

Wilfred had used the magical map to travel around Australia in his shiny new Rugby, and later, he adventured to far away places and countries Grandad had not even heard of.

Grandad read the journal to the boys and they sat at his feet fascinated with every word.

Wilfred explained how the magical map worked. You had to hold the map in front of you and ask it to show you what you wanted.

The map would point a little arrow in the direction you needed to go, and as you travelled in that direction, the map would change and keep directing you until you got there.

It was like an ancient, magical GPS that operated on the desires of the heart.

Wilfred had used it to find his true love, Harriet. He had held the map, and asked it to show him the way to his true love. It had led him to the local convenience store where Harriet worked for her father.

The map was never wrong. Grandad decided that he and the boys should go on a great adventure of their own.

Chapter Sixteen - Betting on the Horse with the Coolest Name

They asked the map to take them on a big mysterious adventure.

The map must have liked this question. The arrow appeared and it was a bright golden arrow pointing to the end of the street.

Grandad and the boys piled into the Rugby and off they went. Dominic held onto the map and told Grandad which way to go when the arrow moved. He didn't know left or right, so he would say, 'Turn your side Grandad', or 'Turn my side.' He was a clever little navigator.

Soon enough they arrived at a mangrove. They all climbed out of the car. Elijah put on his rain boots and led the way. He was very brave and insisted on going first. He picked up a big stick and poked and prodded everything in their path to make sure it was not dangerous.

After walking for a while, the arrow turned into a big red cross and the words 'Dig Here' appeared on the map. Dominic took their buckets and spades from his back pack.

They all dug and after digging a very deep hole, Elijah screamed out.

'My found something Grandad!' His face lit up.

He had in his hand a golden sphere. It looked like some sort of puzzle, music box or treasure box. It was about the size of an orange. Grandad took a closer look but couldn't figure it out.

They took the treasure back home to Nanny. Nanny knew everything. Surely, she would know how to open the magical ball.

When they got home, they told nanny about where the magical map had taken them on their great adventure. She looked over the magical sphere. She could not see any keyholes or writing on the sphere. It just had strange pictures and symbols.

She did a 'Google' search on the internet and finally she found something. The sphere looked like something from an exhibition in London. It was from the site of the ancient Mayans. The Mayans were rumoured to have known the secrets of the stars.

The sphere had been a mystery for many years. There was a great robbery in 1947 and it hadn't been since.

Grandad and the boys thought of Wilfred. He seemed like the sort of larrikin who would do something like that so they went back to the journal.

The last half of the journal had no writing on it. It had seemed to stop very suddenly. Nanny thought it might be in invisible ink. If he had stolen the sphere, he probably didn't want anyone to know about it. Nanny knew a lot about invisible ink. She was a schoolteacher and she taught her class how to write with invisible ink just last week.

She took out a candle and carefully waved the journal lightly above the flame. As if by magic, the words started to appear.

They all sat down and read the rest of the journal. Wilfred had stolen the sphere. The map had led him there and said it was important. He had snuck it back home and had tried all sorts of things to open the sphere. He asked the map what was in the sphere.

The map wrote back 'Every truth a man should know. Every secret, that ever was. Every answer to every question.'

When he asked the map how to open the sphere, it would only reply.

'You must know the truth. You must know the secret. You must know the question before you can have the answer.'

Elijah was holding the sphere. He'd found it so it was agreed that it was his special treasure as the map was Dominic's. Elijah always had the most profound answer to any question so Nanny bent down and looked into his big blue eyes. He was only three but he was an old soul.

Nanny asked Elijah 'What do you think is the truth?'

Elijah considered the answer. 'The truth is good. Be good.' He said in his lisp.

Nanny asked Elijah 'What do you think is the secret?'

Elijah considered the answer. 'The secret is something special. You can't tell anyone the secret because it is a secret. It's in your heart.' He nodded knowingly. He was sure of this one. It was easy.

Nanny asked the last question, 'What do you think the question is?'

Elijah thought about it. He puzzled and then he said ever so firmly, 'Where do you want to go? That's the question. Isn't it?'

The sphere turned in his hands and opened up like a flower. It was made of delicate golden petals on the outside and silver petals on the inside. Inside the sphere was a small leather pouch. It had a picture of the map on the cover. This was the map's home.

Chapter Sixteen - Betting on the Horse with the Coolest Name

At last, they understood what the map and the sphere were telling them.

The map showed you your journey but could not take it for you. The map showed you the adventure and it led you to wherever you wanted to go, but you had to choose where your destination would be.

The joy of an adventure was the discovery and the journey. That was the answer to the secret. Within every person lies their own secret, their own map, and their own adventure.

The boys kept the map safe in its home and took great care of their treasure. The map and sphere had found its way into their hands for a reason. Sometimes the logic of a child's mind is the only way to see the clarity of what has always been right in front of you.

When you look over your life you'll recall many life changing events, births, marriages, first day of school, university, first house, and possibly others not so pleasant - divorce, deaths, bankruptcy.

Everyone is unique but we all experience some major events that are similar. As you look over those life-changing events, you will notice that the majority are 'heart' decisions.

Heart decisions such as marriage, starting a family or buying a house are the ones that logically should have a meticulous plan. More often than not, we go into them blindly and are often surprised when things don't roll quite how we saw it in our vision of blissful Utopia.

Even though you will not feel like it. When you are making major life changing decisions and especially when it's regarding a matter of the heart, you need to look at your expectations objectively and communicate them with anyone else who will be involved in that decision.

As I discussed earlier, we each have our own filters, belief system, and our own cultural learning. What one may consider a reasonable expectation, another may view completely differently.

Every little girls dreams of growing up and wearing a princess dress on her big day. A marriage is not a wedding. A wedding is not a marriage. So much planning goes into that one-day, but none into the marriage itself.

Every significant life changing experience should have a plan. In real estate, I found that people spent more time pondering what to watch on television, than they did on buying their first home or organising their finances.

I know that I am guilty of it too. I jumped in thoughtlessly with many of my own major events. Life planning means that you have to take a step back, and really be honest with yourself and anyone else involved.

You will need to communicate openly and honestly with some subjects that may be uncomfortable. At some point these topics will come up and while you don't want to discuss them while your rose coloured glasses are on, this is actually the best time to do it, rather than when a conflict arises.

Some questions that you can discuss with your partner or consider if you are single are:

What sort of relationships do you want?

If you are getting married, what roles will you both have within the marriage?

What expectations do you have?

You need to communicate this clearly and be very specific. One of you may assume that monogamy is a given part of the deal while the other might have other plans.

What changes will you make?

Marriage is a different dynamic to your previous relationship. How will this affect you?

Will you change your name?

Will you have a prenuptial agreement? These are becoming more popular and should really be a legal necessity when you get married.

Whilst you are in love, you don't want to think anything will ever happen, but contingency planning is necessary and if you pre-plan, it will avoid any future conflicts.

Chapter Sixteen - Betting on the Horse with the Coolest Name

You are two different people with different values, beliefs and assumptions, and your financial planning and expectations will differ. You will need to be very clear on each other's role within the marriage.

When you have children, your life will change again.

Everything you thought would happen in your ideal world of 'when I have kids' is most likely not going to be even remotely similar to the reality.

Raising children is probably the other most popular cause for conflict. We all have vastly different views on what we want for our own family.

Of course, everyone loves babies and many will not tell you about the downsides. Small humans are hard work. They are rewarding and you will love them dearly, but there will be days where you will want to find a nice nunnery and drop the little treasure off Moses style.

If you or your partner falls pregnant, you will hear every birth story and a compendium of conflicting advice from well meaning onlookers. The best advice will come from friends who don't actually have children but are experts in the fields of child rearing and will tell you exactly how to raise your wee one.

As a woman, you will be subject to an immense pressure to have a natural birth and breastfeed until the child is twenty. You will feel as if a failure if you have a caesarean and be frowned upon for giving your child brain damage should the milk not be 'home grown'.

If someone around you is having a child, be conscious of how you communicate with her.

Some women are fortunate enough to experience a natural birth. Others are not. Some find breastfeeding fulfilling. Others cannot feed, or have to bottle feed for other reasons.

Many professionals in the industry put an incredible pressure on women to conform to the current trend or expert advice and add unnecessary pressure.

You are bringing a child into the world and already you will be experiencing a monumental change in your life and they overlook the absolute most important part of raising a healthy child. Your relationship with your child is the most important element of raising that child to be healthy.

If you have a caesarean that is fine if that is what is best for you and your child. Whether you breast feed or bottle feed, that is the right decision based on you and the relationship with your child.

When others give you their advice or their opinions, politely thank them and do what you feel is best. If they persist in their judgements and pressure, be confident and ask them to leave so that you can spend time with your child.

Most people mean well when they interfere and everyone thinks you should do things their way. It gives us a little satisfaction and joy to know someone is taking our advice or someone does something the same way we did it. It is not always welcome. Be aware of this too when you find yourself giving advice. It may not be welcome. Give it only when it is invited.

In Part Three of this book, I will give you some tools for mapping and planning that will help you discuss your values, plans, beliefs and expectations.

Go through the exercises separately at first. If there is more than one person involved, compare your individual maps and afterwards, work on one together.

Consider all your ideas, wishes, and aspirations. Ask yourself why you are taking that path in the first place. Ask yourself what tools you will use to get there. Ask yourself what could go wrong and what you will do if it does. Ask yourself how you will communicate it with others.

When you are done, show it to the other person involved if there is someone, and work on a joint one together. Negotiate outcomes and expectations and have a plan. Have some rules and guidelines and have a clear method of communicating with each other if something comes up later that neither of you had anticipated.

You may find that you are at a point in your life where you are making some very real decisions. You may have had a niggling in your heart that you have been avoiding for some time. You may be on the verge of choosing a different path for yourself.

Not all life-changing choices are happy ones but they are often for the greater long term good. Sometimes you know that you have to do something but fear the short-term repercussions of that decision.

Listen to your heart. Be truthful with yourself. You have a courage within you that you may not have known was there but it will show itself when you need it most.

Plan what you ideally want in your life. Make the decision to follow it when you are ready. Have an action plan. Have a support network. Have mentors and guides.

At first, it will feel mechanical and impersonal planning life's big moments, but as you get a feel for it, it will help you manage your life and it is a fun activity to go back to and review. Your life plan is a living document and one that should evolve and grow as you do.

Try It!

Vision boards are especially effective in the major life elements such as a dream house or an ideal partner or a holiday.

Get a big piece of cardboard and a glue stick and some magazines and scissors. Cut out pictures and visual representations of your ideal world. Cut out words that represent your ideals and paste them all over your board. Put the board up where you will see your vision every day, and you will soon find it will magically start becoming your reality as you focus and move towards your vision.

Our sight comprehends more than any other sense which is one of the major reasons vision boards are so effective.

By planning and communicating, you can simplify your life and prepare for expected outcomes.

PART THREE

TOOLS FOR CHANGE

Chapter Seventeen

The Road Beyond the One I Left Behind

Taking Action

Chapter Seventeen

"It's better to do one job well than two jobs... not so well"

Farmer Pickels – Bob the Builder

The Black family were like any ordinary family. Chaos and danger lurked on every corner and broken toys were a constant threat.

The Black family had a secret though. The children discovered their mother had powers… SUPER Powers. If a toy was broken, all she needed was a butterknife and Shazam, the toy was working again.

The boys thought their mum was the superest mum who ever lived.

One day a spider threatened their very existence. They were preparing for their bath and it menaced its way across the bathroom floor. The boys yelled for mum and Shazam, she'd caught the hairy legged beast in a glass jar and was swiftly showing him the door. Nothing could penetrate the fortress of The Magic Jelly Bean Clubhouse, at least not while Supermum was on the job.

Danger tried to infiltrate the Clubhouse but Mum was always on the alert. If one of the boys hurt his finger, Mum always had a magic kiss that seemed to heal any pain. If one of the boys was feeling sad, she knew just the right song to sing that would make him feel safe and warm. If the dog was looking bare and the boys were making her a superdog costume, Mum always had a ball of string to help turn an ordinary towel into a super cape. Mum was amazing.

There seemed to be no limit to her powers…at least not when they were around.

When the boys weren't home, she was just an ordinary woman, but when they were under her watchful eye, the powers seemed to emerge and she'd spring into action.

When women fall pregnant and have a child, they don't know about the secret society they get inducted to. When the midwife hands you your baby, she also gives you a power. From that moment forward, everything seems dangerous to your beloved bundle, and you will discover powers you never knew existed within yourself.

The Supermum of the Magic Jelly Bean Clubhouse wasn't the only woman with these powers. Her mother had them before here and every other mother had them too. Shazam!

Chapter Seventeen - The Road Beyond the One I Left Behind

When I was a little girl, my parents used to drag me to church, and I spent the bulk of my time looking towards the back where there was a replica of Michelangelo's 'The Pieta'.

I always thought she was so beautiful and graceful. I could stare at it for hours. I did not know the story of it, but saw it through the eyes of a child who appreciates pretty things. I had freckles. I was an ugly duckling so I would wish that one day I would be as pretty as the lady in the church.

As I grew up, I was teaching myself to paint and sculpt and read some pieces on the history of art and Michelangelo's work.

Once again, The Pieta crossed my path. I had not thought of her in years. I saw it this time through a different set of eyes – those of an artist appreciating the perfection and skill of creating soft drapery out of marble.

I read in one of my books that it was the only sculpture that he signed.

When I had my children, I looked at it again through the eyes of a mother.

I was raised Roman Catholic so was familiar with the story of Jesus and Mary by that stage, and looking at her through the eyes of a mother, all I could think was 'She's so serene. If I ever had to hold my own son as she did, I don't think I'd be quite so composed.'

There is a popular tale that when Michelangelo was asked how he created such things of beauty out of stone, he replied,

> 'I didn't do anything. God put Pieta and David in the marble. They were already there. I only had to carve away the parts that kept you from seeing them!'

An artist will see the world differently and interpret it with a combination of skills they have learned coupled with the tools they use for their particular art form.

A chisel in the hands of a skilled carpenter can carve an elegant piece. A chisel in the hands of a baker will be of little value. The skill itself is a tool that will develop over many years. By applying the right tools to the right job with repeated effort, and learning from mistakes, progress and artistic mastery evolves.

The following chapters will cover some tools you can use in your own life to master change and plan your journey.

I will suggest some tools and their uses. You can then choose which ones will suit your needs.

Create your own recipe for your own culinary masterpiece and enjoy the delicate flavours that emerge. Smell the aromas of potential and then taste the sensations of new realities as they unfold before you.

Try to do the exercises at least once. Some of them need to be experienced for full clarity. Choose which fit your personal preferences best.

Now it is time to get your hands dirty. Make sure you have your journal and pens ready, as you will need them in the following chapters.

Try It!

A good place to start is to write out a list of what you have learned so far. Write down notes on the previous chapters and how they relate to you.

Create a bullet list using keywords that describe what changes you would like to make and what long-term benefits you will get when you achieve them.

Writing out your goals gives them a life and increases your chances of achieving them.

Chapter Eighteen

Atlantis isn't Lost - We Are

Your Treasure Map to Utopia

Chapter Eighteen

"To map out a course of action and follow it to an end requires courage"

Ralph Waldo Emerson

Captain Garr was picking food out of his teeth with his knife.

'Moreton....MORETONNNN...' He bellowed to his first.

Moreton came running in. Captain Garr had a reputation for his ferocious temper.

Garr wasn't the smartest pirate on the planet, and he was very impulsive. He always lost his treasure soon after burying it and had to keep borrowing from his famous dad. His dad had cemented his own reputation as the greatest pirate of all time.

Desperate to prove himself as a capable pirate and a legend in his own skin, Garr was determined that this last haul would be the one that would make his name known everywhere. It was an impressive haul. It had taken the crew seven days to unload and bury it and now he was waiting on his cartographer to create the most beautiful treasure map that ever there was.

This voyage would become legend for centuries to come. Songs would praise his honour and his great treasure would be famous. Garr hated waiting though. He had sent Moreton to check on the mapmaker every half hour since they'd set back out to sea.

'IS IT FINISHED YET?' he bellowed.

'Not yet sir,' Moreton replied.

'THIS IS JUST NOT GOOD ENOUGH. I WANT IT NOW.'

With that, Garr made his way to the mapmaker's cabin where he was toiling lovingly over the delicate map detailing the whereabouts of the greatest fortune known to man.

The mapmaker looked up from his work.

'WELL?' Garr bellowed.

'WHEN WILL IT BE FINISHED?'

The mapmaker told him it would take at least seven days…as he had already told him fifty times before. It might even take longer because he was being disturbed every half hour, but he didn't dare say it aloud.

Garr threw his knife at the cabin door in a fit of rage.

'WE NEED A NEW MAP MAKER MORETON.'

'Why captain?' Moreton asked.

'BECAUSE THIS ONE JUST DIED.' With that he ran the poor mapmaker through and tossed him overboard.

Garr's temper had once again cost him his great fortune. Without a map to get back to the island and the treasure, or a mapmaker who knew how to get there, it was once again lost for eternity. When Garr realised what he had done, he went into an awful rage.

Moreton made his way up to the deck and turned the boat around. He had the map to Garr Senior's place but he didn't need it. He knew the way by heart.

To begin any journey, you need a starting point and a destination. It's time to dive into your backpack and pull out the tools I asked you bring earlier.

Take out your pen and your notebook.

Draw a large circle that fills up most of the page. Break this circle into eight segments.

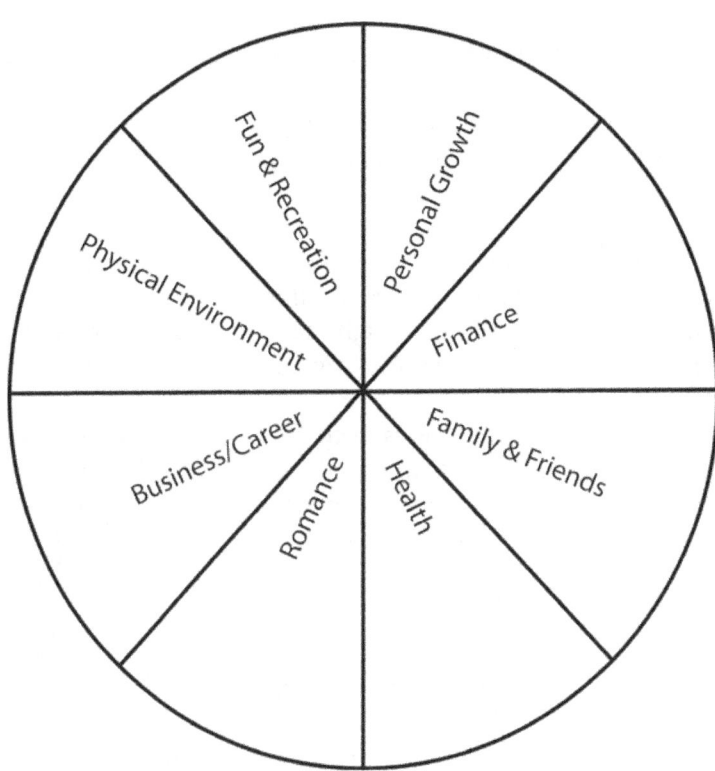

Figure 18.1 - Life Wheel

Draw a line straight down the middle through the centre vertically and another straight across the middle through the centre horizontally. Break the quadrants in half so you now have a wheel like the one in image 18.1.

Write the following inside each segment:
- Family and Friends
- Health
- Finances
- Business/Career
- Physical Environment
- Fun and Recreation
- Personal Growth
- Romance

When using the 'life wheel', usually as a self assessment, you would rate where you think your life is at present in each of those segments. I prefer to use it as a guideline for more detailed planning.

Set the journal aside for now and I will discuss the process of mind mapping.

Tony Buzan first brought the concept of mind mapping to light. He discovered that, as the mind does not think in the linear mode that is common in schools, creating thought maps using keywords and a more organic process allowed free thinking and stimulated innovation and creativity.

The purpose of a mind map is to create an overview and structure to your thoughts. I often start with a hard copy and then later translate it to a neat little printout using mind-mapping software. I use 'freemind'. You can download this 'open source' free tool at :

http://freemind.sourceforge.net

You can use your notebook for the mind maps or if you are feeling a bit arty, use the blank side of a giant piece of wrapping paper or butchers paper. To start each mind map, write your core topic in a bubble in the middle of the page (see figure 18.2).

Figure 18.2 - CentreTitle Bubble for Mind Map

Chapter Eighteen - Atlantis isn't Lost - We Are

From there, create little branches and bubbles off it with sub categories. Just go with the flow. Some people like to put their words into bubbles and others prefer to write along the branches. There is no right or wrong way. Just do what comes naturally. I'm a 'bubble' girl myself but I used both methods in the mind map in figure 18.3.

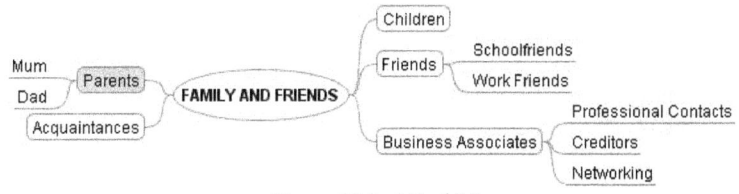

Figure 18.3 - Mind Map

Your sub categories will have sub categories of their own. It's an organic process and you will find some topics will trigger others.

You can do a separate mind map for each of the categories from your wheel.

If that is too complex, you could do just three under the categories of 'Mind- Learning and Career', 'Body – Physical Environment' & 'Spirit – Development and Wellbeing' as most of the other categories will fit into any of these.

Within each of these elements, you currently perform certain roles or have priorities. For instance, in the 'family and friends segment', you might be a mother, a daughter, a sister, a friend, an acquaintance, a mentor, a student, a group leader, a teacher etc.

If you have more than one child, your 'mother' bubble will have a bubble for each of those children, as your relationship with each of them will be different.

If you have a partner, you can put them in this category too if you like, although there is a dedicated category for romance.

Spend some time doing this exercise. Go through each segment of the wheel and mind map them all. When you are finished you will have what looks like a bit of a mess, but what is actually the beginnings of a map of who you are.

If you're having trouble thinking of sub-categories for your elements, some starters are:

Family and Friends

- Mother
- Father
- Son
- Daughter
- Sister
- Brother
- Friend
- Acquaintance
- Mentor
- Group Leader
- Teacher
- Student
- Leader

Health

- Fitness
- Self Defence
- Diet
- Breathing
- Relaxation
- Yoga
- Skincare

Finances

- Budget
- Property Investing
- Stock Trading
- Derivatives
- Self Managed Superannuation
- Financial Advice

Business/Career

- Education
- Further Learning
- Career
- Business Opportunities
- Hobbies that are profitable
- Growth
- Long Term Aspirations
- What do I enjoy doing that might bring me some money
- Past jobs
- Past Experience
- Skills
- What can you outsource?

Physical Environment

- House
- Car
- Housekeeper or help
- Furniture
- Where you live
- Type of property

Fun and Recreation

- Hobbies
- Outdoor Activities
- Skills
- Music
- Arts
- Crafts
- Dancing

Personal Growth

- Self Development
- Learning
- Growing
- Charity
- Religion
- Spirituality

Romance

- Your partner if you have one
- Ideal lover
- How do you want to be treated?
- How will you treat your loved one'
- What will he/she look like?
- Physical Attributes?
- Personality Traits
- Do you want a partner?
- Sexuality – what are you preferences?
- What's important in a relationship?
- What sort of relationship do you want?

It is a fun exercise and should not be laborious.

Some of them will be confronting but as you do the exercises, don't do it with the perspective that anyone is going to see them.

Whenever we do these exercises, we are still conscious of judgement or think ahead and consider showing someone to get an outward approval.

Write the first maps with the mindset that only you will see it. If you want to show someone later, that is fine but for now, our intention is that only you will see it. This will keep judgements at bay and help the process.

Try It!

To add an extra dimension to your maps, I will draw on an NLP principle called 'modelling'. By modelling the behaviours and traits of people who are successful in any field, it is apparent that the same results are possible in others.

I am going to use modelling now and ask you to go back to your mind maps. In each of the bubbles, as you go through, ask yourself who you admire that is presently filling that role or 'who does this well?'

Write those names in separate bubbles. Use a separate colour if you have one. You may not find a model for each of your bubbles and that's fine, but somewhere in your life, there are people you admire for various reasons, be it a sportsperson, a business mentor, a famous actor, a spiritual leader or maybe even your own mother.

Somewhere in your life is someone you admire, or many people you admire. See where they fit in your map and put them in.

For each of those bubbles with the names of your mentors, create more bubbles with the traits that you admire about them and why you admire them.

After you have mapped your mentors, go through and add any bubbles for your desires – What do you want in your ideal world and life?

Be honest and be imaginative.
This is your life and your world.

Chapter Nineteen

You Put your Right Leg In

You Put your Right Leg Out

How can you Change your Life
using Simple Business Principles?

Chapter Nineteen

"Would you like fries with that?"

The pimply faced boy at the second window

Back in the 60's a couple of Beatniks were having a philosophical discussion over a friendly bong.

'You know man, like; we need to start a bank for the people.'

Gurgle… gurgle…gurgle…

'Oh yeah. Like, with no rules and no fees and people like us working there so everyone is all about the love.'

Gurgle… gurgle…gurgle…

…and so the conversation continued as the beatniks hashed out their business plan. (Ha ha...get it 'hashed'). As they never quite saw any reason to come down from their permanent state of bliss, they ran with it.

All their friends thought it was a great idea, and everyone decided to work free because it was the bank built on love.

Soon people started to take notice and liked the idea of a bank without rules or fees so they started to put their money in the bank. Because there were no rules or guidelines, they decided to keep the systems simple.

Customers would bring in their deposits, the bank staff would put it in a bag and write the persons first name on it and then put it in the big lock up room out the back.

It was perfect. The customers loved how the staff would give them a hug before they left.

Soon the cracks started to show. Customers started coming to withdraw their money and sometimes there would be more than one bag with the same name on it.

The two Beatniks decided it was time to call a business meeting.

Gurgle…gurgle…gurgle…

'Man, I think we're screwed.'

Gurgle…gurgle…gurgle…

By applying business principles to your daily life – systems and processes, you can simplify your life and achieve consistent outcomes.

If you recognised that most stress comes from a feeling of losing control, not having enough time and living in chaos, you can use a systematic business process to manage your life and have more time to do the things you enjoy.

If you have decided to go into business for yourself, systems and procedures are necessary. When you read business books, you will find there are some parallels that you can apply to your day-to-day life.

Most business books will draw your attention to McDonalds being the perfect business model. Every facet of a McDonalds business has a documented manual that is systematic and easily adapted by an unskilled worker in a relatively short period. As a result, there is a consistent and predictable outcome.

In the reference section at the back of the book, you will find more recommended reading on business processes. I will now draw on the necessity of systems and their application to life management.

Building your life and businesses around systems and rituals is not a new philosophy. Rituals have been around for centuries and they are the foundations of every religion. Some religions have used their knowledge of the power of ritual to influence en-mass to their own ends, but regardless of the motivation, the outcomes are always the same, which is why it is still one of the most effective ways of managing your day to day life as well as your business.

Chapter Nineteen - You Put your Right Leg In. You Put your Right Leg Out

When structuring a business plan, or life plan, the first thing you need to do is differentiate between projects and the processes. A project has a beginning, middle and an end and a process is an ongoing activity.

A project is something you will do once or a major core element. A process can be a part of a project. It will be a systemised activity. You can teach it to another person. They can follow it for a predictive outcome.

A **project** is a noun – a *'thing'* and a **process** is a verb – a *'doing word'*.

An example would be if you wanted to compete in the Tour De France. That will be a project. To complete the project, you will train for 2 hours a day. You will eat well. You will follow daily processes that will help you complete the project.

Another example would be if you wanted to start your own online business. You will need a website. That will be a project. You will also need to set up and follow daily tasks to maintain your business, such as stock ordering, answering emails etc. They are processes. Setting up these processes will be a project.

Most successful business people, sportspeople and influencers have success habits - daily habits they follow to achieve super-human results. The next process will help you formulate your path to succeeding and reaching your true potential and living your ideal.

Try It!

Managing projects is easy when you have the right tools. To add structure to your project I will illustrate with my own little acronym. It wouldn't be a self-development book without my own acronym.

Let me introduce you to OTAR©. OTAR© stands for:

- *Outcomes*
- *Tasks*
- *Actions*
- *Review*

I'll cover these more thoroughly:

Outcome - To have a ritual, you need to have a desired outcome that you want to achieve repeatedly. So using the NLP (Neuro Linguistic Programming) tool of starting with the end in mind, define your outcome. I usually do a small bullet list of the key outcomes I wish to achieve and then summarise them into a single paragraph.

Tasks are projects you will need to undertake to achieve this outcome. The first task is always to mind map and do a brainstorming session.

Actions are the processes you will use to achieve the outcome. Actions will be measurable by the results they deliver. All actions will have a pre-determined result.

Review – as your plans evolve and change, you will need to periodically review your progress to see if it's still relevant, recognise what is and isn't working and make any changes.

A guideline is on the next page. Keep a copy of this nearby when you work through your mind maps in the next chapter.

OTAR© Model

Outcome

- What is the purpose of the meeting/Project?
- What is the desired outcome?

Tasks

- Note the tasks required to achieve the outcome.
- Prioritise Tasks.
- How are you going to measure them?

Actions

- Collate notes from tasks into required actions
- Each action should specify:
  - **What** - *What is the task?*
  - **Where** - *Does it require a specific location? Where does it fit into the overall picture?*
  - **When** - *What is the timeframe for achieving the task?*
  - **Why** - *Why is it necessary?*
  - **How** - *How will we achieve it – This should be a step by step schedule*
  - **By Whom** - *What tasks should you be doing? Where is your time best spent?*
- Can you outsource to someone else to best leverage your time?
- Would it be cost prohibitive to do this?
- What is your time worth?

Review

- How and when will you measure your results? Are any changes necessary?

Chapter Twenty

One Two Buckle my Shoe

Developing Daily Success Habits

Chapter Twenty

Alice: Would you tell me, please, which way I ought to go from here?
The Cat: That depends a good deal on where you want to get to
Alice: I don't much care where.
The Cat: Then it doesn't much matter which way you go.
Alice: ...so long as I get somewhere.
The Cat: Oh, you're sure to do that, if only you walk long enough.

Alice in Wonderland – Lewis Carroll

Willow and Jade were conjoined twins. They shared most of their vital organs so could never be separated. Willow had control of their left arm and heart and Jade controlled the right hand side and lower part of their body.

They always knew they were different and they came from a loving home where they were supported and encouraged to grow and develop their own interests.

They fought and disagreed as most siblings do and even though they shared much of their bodies, they were as different as any two girls could be.

As the girls grew, Jade started to become more conscious of herself but Willow just accepted life as it was and always saw the beauty of life.

Jade was wild and rebellious and Willow was quiet and subdued. When Jade looked in the mirror she saw pain and was resentful that she wasn't like other girls. Willow saw a beautiful sister and thought it was so wonderful that they were always so close, especially so she could keep a watchful eye on her as she could be a little reckless at times.

The sisters managed to overcome many obstacles over their lives. Their friends loved them dearly and they each had their own social groups and learned to negotiate rather well. Sometimes Jade's form of negotiation involved sulking or bullying her sister but in the end they did work out their differences and usually came to an agreement.

Willow considered herself habitually lucky. Jade wondered why she had been dealt such a challenging life.

When the sisters were nearing their thirtieth birthday, Jade started experiencing pain in her lower abdomen. The doctors told the girls they couldn't operate and they did not have long to live. Jade was inconsolable but Willow told her why she was thankful for the gifts she'd been given.

> 'When others have lost their loved ones, you see the heartache in their eyes that they can't go too. We will always be together to look after each other, even in the afterlife.'

> 'I've always admired you and loved that when I've cried, I need only turn my head and you are there to whisper words of strength in my ear.'

> 'I've always looked at other girls and seen them struggling with their looks and their weight and worrying over trivial matters. We were always lucky. We had each other. We've always had our own little club.'

> 'When you have cried and wanted to be like other girls, I have thought how empty I would be without you by my side.'

The girls spent the last of their days living life and enjoying every beauty this world had to offer. They were grateful for every day they had. Jade knew the riches she had with her quiet sibling and was no longer afraid. Her only regret was that she had not known it sooner.

Chapter Twenty - One Two Buckle my Shoe

How do you tie a shoelace? We don't really think about it now because once we have done a repeated action every day, it becomes a habit and we do it on autopilot. I do however remember the very first time I tied my shoelace.

If you ask my mother, she will tell you that as a child, I may have perhaps been a little bit stubborn; just a little tiny bit. I may also have had a temper.

One morning when I rose from bed, I decided that that day, I was going to tie my own shoelaces. Nothing could change my mind. I was going to tie them myself. It was not negotiable.

I remember sitting at the bottom of the stairs. I was in my school uniform and mum was rushing us out the door to get to school on time. I had been sitting there trying to tie my shoelaces for a good while already but I was determined. Mum tried to do them so we could leave, so I threw a tantrum as only I knew how.

I tried it once. I tried it twice. Mum sat down and explained it to me, and I tried again. Finally, I tied my shoelace. After many tears and frustration, I had done it. Now, I had to tie the other one. The second took a bit of effort too, but we did get to school sometime that day.

The first and second time you do something, it can be frustrating and it can take you out of your comfort zone.

As children we are so eager to learn and to grow up that we don't worry about the failures, we just keep trying. We fall off our bike, skin our knees and eventually learn to ride. As time goes by and we grow up and that curiosity fades. We forget the pride that swells within us when we achieve something that was at first unfamiliar.

If you create a system and a formula and practice it daily, it becomes a habit. Soon it will feel like second nature and you will not have to think consciously. At first, it may be uncomfortable.

It's shown repeatedly that the best sportspeople, business people and most successful people are those who practice daily success habits with an absolute focus.

The most effective habits to reach your goals are:

- A positive mental attitude
- Commitment
- Discipline
- Self confidence
- Persistence
- Focus
- Creativity
- A business mind (not taking things personally)
- An ability to see the lesson or benefits in any situation
- A clear intention of your desired outcome
- An emotional belief and passion in what you are trying to achieve

Try It!

I have found that by creating a list of daily success habits, you can quickly achieve more in a small amount of time.

I change my list regularly. I find that it takes about 3 months of repetition to become a firm habit. Every three months I review my list, and I remove the ones that have become well-formed habits. I now take them for granted as a daily activity. I then add some new unfamiliar tasks and repeat the process.

Some of your chosen habits will be permanent ones or longer term, but some of them you can rotate or update. To develop your own success habits, have a look through your mind maps and focus on the traits, roles or ambitions that you have listed in each category as your higher priorities.

Start by looking at the 'wheel' we constructed earlier. Being that it is a circle and a wheel metaphor, the common assumption is that to achieve harmony and balance in your life, you have to focus on every element in equal measure. This is not so. Health may be important to you and spirituality only of mild interest. If this is the case, then prioritise it as such.

Chapter Twenty - One Two Buckle my Shoe

Start by prioritising the order of importance of the elements in your life. Number each segment from one to eight in order of its level of importance and priority in your own life. This will help you create your first list of success habits. Don't try to do too many at first. You can build it up later, but for now, just create a small list.

To create the 'shortlist', select the map for your number one segment and on a separate piece of paper, list your top three priorities.

Go through each segment in order and repeat the process, listing just the top three priorities from each life segment. When you are done, you will now have a list of twenty-four priorities.

From here, go through and select a few that you want to focus on. It doesn't matter how many from each category. Just go through the list and pick any that you feel strongly about.

You have the maps to come back to over time as you review and change but for now, just focus on a select few topics or traits that you really want to focus on and strengthen.

Once you have chosen your topics, traits or priorities, create a project for each using the OTAR© formula we covered in the last chapter.

Using one of my own priorities as an example, I'll illustrate how I use the OTAR© model.

The priority I have chosen is *'Write a book'*.

I have 'marketing the book' and 'editing the book' and other topics as sub bubbles on my maps, so they are not a priority or part of this task. For now, the topic I am going to focus on is 'Write a Book'.

To start to define my habits and processes, I need to define my desired outcome.

You can use a mind map to do this if you like. I just start with a few keywords and create a bullet list. The list will usually be the elements I want to cover in this project:

- Write a book:
- Topic:
- Target Audience:
- Purpose:
- Completed by:
- Time taken:

From your bullet list or mind map, create a small paragraph of your ideal outcome.

Mine will be:

> *'To write a complete manuscript, on the topic of personal development to assist people in managing their lives and priorities. The purpose of the book will be to give my readers the tools to structure their lives, alleviate stress, and achieve their desires and dreams. The first draft of the manuscript will be completed by this close of this week and I will write it in extended sittings of complete uninterrupted, focus and concentration.'*

Your Outcome statement is a clear, definitive statement.

If you have a business, the entire process we have covered so far is a great tool for creating your Unique Selling Proposition, Mission Statement or Vision Statement. It is a way of 'chunking down' your vision with a sharp, defined focus.

The next part of the OTAR© is the 'Tasks' - Tasks are projects.

The first project is to mind map and think in steps working backwards from your end vision.

Think ahead to when the Outcome is a reality and complete. It is done, and everything's in place. Now think backwards on the steps of how you got there. There will have been some small projects along the way. Like stepping stones, they will take you from where you are now. Track the journey backwards from when you have finished the project.

Mind map these steps. A little sidenote; during this step, remember to include rewards for yourself as you achieve each milestone.

With my topic, some of my steps working backwards from my desired outcome will be:

- Saving the file and printing it out.
- Taking breaks periodically.
- Writing all my thoughts in a free flow session
- Removing distractions – e-mail, phones, social media and telling everyone in advance that I am writing and am not to be disturbed
- Creating a block of time to write
- Creating a clean, uncluttered environment and having water and the resources needed nearby.
- Prioritising my chapter tree and keywords
- Creating a chapter tree and keywords as prompts
- Mind mapping all the topics I wish to cover in my book.

Some of these will be projects, and some will be processes. Differentiate which is which by writing 'PJ' beside the projects and 'PS' beside the processes. Define the projects first and created a pointed list in start to finish order.

My projects will be:

- Mind Mapping all the topics I wish to cover in my book
- Creating a chapter tree and keywords as prompts
- Prioritising my chapter tree and keywords
- Creating a clean, uncluttered environment and having water and the resources needed nearby.
- Creating a block of time to write
- Removing distractions – e-mail, phones, social media and telling everyone in advance that I am writing and am not to be disturbed

I will define a paragraph for each, much like my outcome statement.

Remeber to look at the original worksheet and ask yourself:
- **What** - *What is the task?*
- **Where** - *Does it require a specific location? Where does it fit into the overall picture?*
- **When** - *What is the timeframe for achieving the task?*
- **Why** - *Why is it necessary?*
- **How** - *How will we achieve it – This should be a step by step schedule*
- **By Whom** - *What tasks should you be doing? Where is your time best spent?*

- Are there any outsourcing possibilities?
- Would it be cost prohibitive to do this?
- What is your time worth?

After defining the projects, create a paragraph for each of your processes. Then go back through the entire OTAR© and pick out some that can be outsourced.

For the ones you want to do yourself, define those that can be broken down into smaller tasks that apply as a daily activity.

If you are writing a book, you may break your writing processes down to writing two pages a day. That is a very simple and achievable task and in just 50 days, you will have 100 pages done.

When the projects and processes are clear and specific, create a review schedule.

When would you like to revisit and review this task?

How will you measure its success?

As you go through each of your priorities, you will see some repeat processes starting to appear. You will see some repeat projects and processes that that you can merge or outsource.

When you have finished all your schedules, you now have a clearly defined path of the projects and processes you need to follow in a systemised and step-by-step format.

The next step will be to pull out all the outsourcing tasks and sign up for your account with the outsourcing site.

Create your advertisements. Present each task as a clearly defined project. Specify your desired outcome. Specify the exact processes that need following, the period and your budget. You are now a manager and you have just cut out a massive chunk of work for yourself. Does your goal seem closer and more attainable now?

With the remaining processes and projects, pick out some to do daily to take you closer to your outcome. Commit each day to doing every single one of those processes for as long as you need.

Managing your time is easy when you appreciate what you can achieve is a small amount of time and when you don't overwhelm yourself with entire projects but instead focus on small actions and processes with an outcome and intent in mind.

As you complete each project or process over time, go back to your mind maps periodically and repeat the processes. Soon you will find you are building up momentum and really making some positive changes in your life.

Chapter Twenty-One

There's a Hole in my Bucket

What are you Worth?

Building Pipelines and Income Streams

Chapter Twenty-One

"Your Pipelines Are Your Lifelines!"

Burke Hedges – The Parable of the Pipeline

Peppy wasn't like the other ducks.

Each day they would file past on their foraging expedition and search for food. He had a gammy leg so couldn't go too far but he also had a sharp mind.

Peppy set about creating a better way to find food. Every day for a week as the others went off to scavenge for food, Peppy stayed back and learned everything he could about gardening and planted seeds. He had decided that he would grow his own food.

After that first week, he was growing hungry as he was nearing the last of the few rations he had left and he almost gave up on his plan, but he was sure it would work so he continued.

He would lovingly tend his garden, and soon the first sprouts started to appear. Peppy cared for his garden day in and day out with the same ritual.

After the second week, two vegetables were ready to eat and that night he ate a feast fit for a king. The other ducks saw Peppy's great meal and wanted some too.

Peppy offered to teach the other ducks how to garden, but it was too much work and they did not want to learn anything new so they continued to go off daily and forage for food.

Soon juicy delicious worms started coming to Peppy's garden too. They like the lush soil he had cultivated and he always left out some spare lettuce leaves so they would come over to munch on them.

Peppy had enough to spare so he started to trade his excess vegetables and juicy worms to the other ducks.

He would swap them for nick knacks and furnishings for his nest.

Peppy soon became a very rich duck, but he never stopped tending to his beloved garden as he had grown to love the ritual as much as the riches it delivered.

The Romans were the great innovators of many fascinating systems that we take for granted now but one of the most amazing discoveries they implemented was the aqueduct and the great invention of plumbing.

Imagine that every time you felt like a drink or a bath, you had to get your bucket and wander down to the stream or the well and carry the water back. I don't know about you, but to be honest, I think I'd be smelly and dehydrated after a couple of days. Screw that!

By spending a little time building a more efficient system, you save time in the long term and get the repeat benefits of that system. The same principle applies to your income.

Most of us have one source of income, being our work or business. Some have investments, which should be bringing in additional income streams. What would happen if you couldn't do the work anymore? What would happen if you lost your primary income stream?

Most of us would be up the creek without a paddle. It's important to establish multiple streams of income so that eventually you do not have to trade your precious time for money anymore.

Setting up these income streams will take effort and time, but they will provide you with repeat benefits and you will usually find they snowball and build momentum over time.

Many of us grow up with an unhealthy view of money and wealth. Our conditioning tells us to associate the desire for money or wealth with greed and envy, yet we all want for more.

In the past, it came from the martyrdom syndrome of the church. Today it comes from an entire social structure built on a hierarchal foundation and taxation system where 'employees' are a necessary element to the overall success of our society.

The teaching in schools and in the media is to aspire to the 'great dream'. Study, get a good job, get a mortgage and a home and enslave yourself for a good 60 years.

Assess your relationship with money. Money can bring many wonderful joys into your life. It can allow you more time with your loved ones. It can give you freedom and opportunity to do the things you love. It can give you the ability to help those less fortunate and it can give you lots of cool 'stuff' if that is what you desire.

When most people start on their journey to acquiring wealth, they don't speak of it to their friends and family for fear of their prejudice or judgement. They work diligently and quietly in the background and when they do acquire wealth, others assume it came easily and can feel envious.

Be confident and don't worry about what anyone thinks of you. If you desire to be free and have choices in your life, you are going to need some dosh to do that.

Over a lifetime, we are trained to believe that we are worth only our salary in our 'good job'. We don't consider what our actual worth is. We measure our wealth by our income and our assets (which are actually liabilities if there's a debt attached to it).

Instead, we should calculate our personal wealth on our opportunities, our skills, our life experience and the riches we can bring to those around us.

Try it!

I know, it sounds like I'm going off on a tangent with my weird hippie love-in here, but work with me, I am going somewhere with this.

Think over your lifetime. What sports have you played? What hobbies have you enjoyed? What pass-times do you enjoy? Do you have a party trick? Do you speak well? What do you do naturally well? What is your personality type? What makes you unique? Every one of us has gifts or talents to which we have always had an affinity and natural aptitude. Think about it.

What do you enjoy doing in your spare time?

What sort of people do you attract in your life?

Are you a systems and processes person or a 'free spirit'? I have found since becoming a systems and processes person that I am actually a lot more spontaneous and free because I know where I have time and what changes are possible in my schedule.

Think about the mistakes you have made. Do you screw everything up? What lessons have you learned about what 'not' to do? You might be someone who has a gift for doing everything the wrong way. That's a good thing too.

Every experience you have had over your lifetime and every talent you hold, every lesson you have learned and everything you enjoy is valuable. When we become good at something, we forget that others are not as proficient as we are. Other people are just starting out. Other people want to learn what we know.

Are you a mother or father?

Do you have a successful relationship with your partner or children?

Do you have any systems or tools that others could use to improve their relationships?

Have you figured out a formula for managing a career and family?

What do others say about you?

Do they say, 'I wish I had, or I wish I could do this as well as you?'

How do you study?

Do you read much?

What sort of books do you read?

Do people come to you to ask you to recommend a movie?

Do you listen to a lot of music?

Your life is worth something. Mind map out everything you can possibly think of about what you have to offer. Go through the questions above and map out as many answers as you can.

Put your name in the centre circle and map yourself out. Include all the mistakes you made and lessons you have learned. Include everything you have spent money on in a pursuit of learning the things that are dear to you.

For instance, if you bought books on how to play the guitar, put it in your mind map. Soon you will start to see that at some point, you spent money on something to learn a skill that you have since learned and adapted well. You might be able to teach someone else how to do that skill or you might be able to develop a product – a video or a book that will do that over and over again after you've spent the initial time in creating the project and processes and outsourced what you can.

There is a wealth of value within you that others need and want to learn and if you are spending time on those things already and enjoying doing them, wouldn't that be nicer than trading your time for the 9-5?

Once you have your mind maps done, create new mind maps for some of your favourite topics and mind map as many ways as you can think of to make money from those talents, gifts and experiences.

Pick one that you would like to focus on. Create an OTAR© and focus on it. Do the tasks you need to do daily to make it happen, and when it is running like a well-oiled machine, go back to your mind maps and pick another.

It is important to do only one at a time or you may burnout. If you are wandering off on tangents, you won't finish one. You will drop all the balls and give up. Just pick one. It is tempting to try to do a few of them and run off with ideas when you see your true value. I know...I have done it myself.

You will get ideas over the coming days when you're driving in your car or walking on the beach. Just take your notebook with you and jot the ideas down. Put them out of mind until you are ready to develop them further.

Don't think them out too thoroughly. Just jot them down as a small mind map or bullet list. When you are ready to choose your next project, come back to it. Just pick one project at a time and the chances of you completing that project and seeing the benefits will increase tenfold.

Document your system as you go. The mind-map and OTAR© journey you are taking to set up the system are a saleable product within themselves. Create system manuals and systematic guidebooks on how to set up an income stream in that field. Voila, you have managed to come up with two products from that single topic.

To do this, I just keep a work log each day by my desk and note the start and finish times and just some bullet steps. When you have completed your project, you can just go back to your logbook, refine it and polish it up and there you have a separate marketable product.

Remember that as you go through and do this, you can always come back and do more as you create more systems and processes and outsource the tasks you don't want to do. You will free up your time and you will build momentum.

As you go through the processes and start seeing the benefits of following your bliss and doing what you love, you will see the TRUE value of your time and your personal value and self worth. Your time is valuable. Treasure it.

Whatever brings you joy is your calling. Where do you lose all concepts of time? Where do you get completely lost in a moment? It doesn't matter what it is. Cast your judgments aside. We are all here for a purpose and every one of us has a different purpose. What you enjoy doing is your calling. Follow it and you will see how wonderful your world is as everything just seems to start magically happening for you.

Chapter Twenty-One - There's a Hole in my Bucket

If you have read this far, chances are you may be enjoying my book. Often when we enjoy a good book, we tell our friends about it. If you were considering telling your friends about my book, you can profit in the exchange.

Word of mouth advertising is so effective because the recommendation comes from a foundation of a trusted relationship and is in your own words.

I am thankful for everyone who shares my book with their friends and would like to reward you for your efforts so if you were going to give me a good wrap, drop over to my website and sign up to my affiliate campaign. I will pay you for every sale that results from your referrals.

You might not be able to retire on it, but it is still an additional income for something you may have been going to do free. If you look at every website you visit, you might find a link in the footer that says 'Affiliate'.

For services you already use and are familiar with, this can be a great stream of additional income. To learn more about my own affiliate campaign, just drop by my website at www.tanyablack.com and click on the link for further details.

Build your multiple pipelines. Learn as much as you can about the topics you love and then teach others. It is your world. It is your life. Choose your own path and make your own decisions.

Chapter Twenty-Two

That's a Cool Bike Does it do Burnouts?

Tools and Resources for Managing Stress and Building Courage

Chapter Twenty-Two

*"Close your eyes and you will see clearly.
Cease to listen and you will hear the truth"*

Paul Wilson 'Completely Calm'

The Summerhills Sanatorium was not like other institutions. The occupants of Summerhills were superheros who had cracked under the various pressures that superness can bring.

The walls were made of lead-lined soundproof cromellium carbonate. The staff all wore meteor fibre gowns (early on some of the Heroes with see-through vision were a bit pervy).

Everything about Summerhills was a little bit different. Many of the heroes had initially enjoyed the attention and applause that their powers had brought them, but soon found that being super could turn sour when the weight of responsibility weighed upon them.

Some had persistent insomnia. Some couldn't handle their super-hearing. The telepaths couldn't quieten their own minds and soon found the negative projections of some people were clouding their own judgements.

The doctors at Summerhills took great care in treating their special patients. Sumerhills was not an asylum. It was a rehabilitation facility.

Many of the superheroes chose to stay on at Summerhills even after they'd found peace. It was so tranquil and was located out in the foothills of the mountains where the sounds of nature and the smells of freedom were a blissful reminder of the beauty of simplicity.

It didn't matter how super you were, almost all superheroes ended up at Summerhills.

When they were still in service, the assumption was that it is the place to go when your career is over, but anyone who had been there would tell you otherwise.

Summerhills was the beginning of something new and fulfilling.

Summerhills was founded by Captain Marvellous. He was the granddaddy of all superheroes. Nobody expected he'd ever fall apart. He had every power imaginable. He had x-ray vision, super strength, telepathy, the power to freeze and the power to make fireballs.

Having such an array of powers was exhausting. He had to control his temper. He couldn't go out drinking with the boys and it was hard finding a super woman. Women threw themselves at Captain Marvellous but he knew none of them would be able to understand the implications of being with a superhero. It was a lonely existence.

Captain Marvellous had finally cracked when he fell in love with a beautiful woman but couldn't return her love. He could read her thoughts and knew she loved him but allowing himself to love her too would only hurt her. After he fell in love with her, he cracked under the pressure of expectation and started making monumental mistakes. He retreated to the mountains. He called on Yogis and Gurus and created Summerhills to help other superfolk.

At first they came in dribs and drabs but soon Summerhills was a retreat of like souls where super was just the norm.

Chapter Twenty-Two - That's a Cool Bike. Does it do Burnouts?

When I had my first son, my step-dad gave me some sage advice. If you get frustrated with your kids, have a look at yourself. The things they do that drive you nuts most likely come from you.

What a prophecy foretold! Every day I learn a lesson from them and often see the answer within myself.

One afternoon, after a long day at work, I was driving home and my two little humans were in the back of the car. We were at a T-intersection behind a silver Four Wheel Drive and I was getting frustrated.

There were three breaks in the traffic and this clown just sat there. So I said to myself 'Come on Dildo'. (I thought about changing that for the book to sound like less of an incompetent parent, but I'm going to tell the truth.)

From the back seat came two little voices, 'Come on Dido. Come on Dido'. I explained to them that mummy wasn't being nice and that was that. Fortunately they couldn't pronounce it. I would have had a rather embarrassing time explaining myself at kindy.

A week later, we were driving to a friend's house. We stopped at the traffic lights, and my three-year-old son looks out his window and notices a silver four wheel drive in the lane next to us. 'Hey look mummy, it's Dido.' Being the friendly lad he is, he gives them a wave and says 'Hi Dido'.

At this point, I thought it time to be a bit more conscious of my communication skills and work on getting some tools to manage stress and frustration.

There are many tools for managing stress and if you look at it from three different perspectives; you will find one or a combination that will work for you.

Firstly, there is the **physical** perspective. Some of the core focuses in this element are breathing, posture, diet, water, exercise, Reflexology, Pressure Points, Kinesiology, Acupuncture and Aromatherapy.

Secondly, there is the **mental** perspective. Some exercises and concentrations in this area are meditation, hypnosis, NLP, Brainwave Entrainment, Psychology and Creative Expression and Autosuggestion.

Lastly, there is the **spiritual** perspective. Spirituality is often confused with Religion. The bulk of your spiritual belief system may stem from your religion but spirituality extends beyond that. If you are not a religious person, you are still a spiritual one.

When you think of your past, be aware of where you view it in relation to your body. You will probably think of it as being behind you but most often, it is not within the body itself. That is your spirit. It has fascinated scholars and philosophers for centuries.

All three of these perspectives have various tools and methodologies you can learn and apply to help you stay in peak condition and be your best self. I will expand on some of the tools I use within each element and summarise each. Most of them have compendiums of books about the given topics but I will capture the outline and supply some tools you can use now in your day-to-day life.

Physical - You may not be aware of how your posture affects your entire physical and mental attitude. Have a look at your posture and notice the posture of those around you. Many programs focus on how to move and hold a posture to minimise effort and pressure on your body, skeleton and organs. An easy way to correct your posture is to imagine you are a string puppet.
Relax your arms, legs and neck and imagine there is a string from the crown of your head. The puppeteer pulls on the sting and when he does your head lifts up, your chin is up, your back is relaxed but straight and your legs fall into place.
When you are sitting, sit with your feet flat on the floor, and imagine the string on your head holding your head up. Look the world in the eyes and you will notice that in doing this and correcting your posture, you will naturally start to feel more confident.
The next exercise is to smile. If you are feeling a bit flat, smile. It doesn't matter if you don't feel like smiling. Just smile. Fake it. Soon you will find that you are actually starting to feel a bit better just from that shift.
Another common physical problem many of us have that causes stress and tension all over your body is clenching your jaw. Relax your jaw. If your jaw is relaxed, the rest of your body falls into alignment. To relax your jaw, press the back tip of your tongue gently against the back of your front top teeth. Your jaw will drop slightly and you will most likely yawn as your body sucks in the oxygen it's missing.

Once your jaw is relaxed and you are feeling calm and your posture is relaxed and your body is in alignment, focus on your breathing. There are many breathing techniques around that can improve your stamina, focus, concentration and various ailments. Most of us don't breathe properly. We breathe into our lungs and not our diaphragm. If you put your hand on your abdomen, you will notice it goes up and down as you breathe. That is where you want the oxygen to go. When you breathe in, your abdomen should rise and when you breathe out, it should contract.

When you breathe in, imagine a coffee plunger pushing the air right down into your diaphragm. Breathe out slowly and watch it go down again. When you breathe this way, the oxygen gets into your blood, increases your alertness, and improves your posture. It is all relative.

Other physical concentrations should be to maintain a healthy diet, drink plenty of water and ensure you have some physical exercise each day. A 15-minute walk is enough to keep you in good shape and gets you out and about too.

Other activities you might consider for their various relaxation benefits are:

- *Reflexology* – using pressure points in the feet hands and ears to manage different stress symptoms.
- *Naturopathy* – Natural medicines and traditional medicines
- *Acupuncture* – A Chinese alternative medical practice using pressure points and fine needles to treat physical ailments
- *Acupressure* – Stimulating pressure points to relieve and treat ailments
- *Aromatherapy* - using fragrances and blends for various conditions
- *Yoga* – relaxation, meditation and stretching.
- *Tai Chi* – physical movement and low impact exercise to achieve calm and physical wellbeing. This is also a spiritual exercise.
- *Massage* – massage stimulates blood cells and oxygen in your body and it feels nice.
- *Sex* – We all know the benefits of sex. I'll throw in a few scientific words to make it sound more acceptable. It releases natural endorphins, and well, that's all I've got...but I have heard it is good for you.

This list is by no means exhaustive. There are many other methodologies and treatments for staying in good physical health, these ones are some of the more common ones that people use.

Mental - Maintaining mental clarity and a positive mindset is something many of us do not do consciously yet it is of the most importance. Mind, body and spirit are all connected and making changes in one element will affect the other two.

If you allow yourself to succumb to stress or get and burned out, you will often find that your body soon packs it in and you get very sick. Many physical symptoms come from a mental trigger.

Think of the way your body responds when you are scared. Your heart races and you might get goose bumps. You sweat.

Think of how your body responds when you think of a lover or your high school crush.

The power of the mind is truly astounding. By having a conscious control over your thoughts and emotions, you are also controlling your physical health.

The placebo effect demonstrates this perfectly. Patients often respond to a sugar pill to treat their illness when they think it is a prescribed medicine. The body responds to what we perceive. It is much the same as the NLP principle of conditioning.

I use two primary tools for maintaining my clarity and focus. They are brainwave entrainment and hypnosis. You can enhance your mental clarity by tapping into your subconscious and by stimulating brain states. There are found brain states:

BETA

The first state is Beta. When your mind is in the Beta state, it is your conscious state of critical thinking. Its application is for peak performance and mental clarity.

ALPHA

The second brain state is Alpha. Alpha is the state you are in when you're driving your car and get those *'aha'* moments. It is often associated with creativity, relaxation and visualisation.

Your body relaxes, you awareness expands. It is a helpful addition to hypnosis. When the shamans used drums to go into a trance and the monks used the drone and hum of their chants, the sounds stimulated an Alpha brain frequency.

THETA
Theta is associated with increased retention, heightened receptivity, subconscious memory, dreamlike states of imagining and inspiration. As you go into a deeper state of hypnosis, you can use affirmations and imagery to impact lasting changes and enhance learning in this state.

DELTA
Delta is associated with deep sleep and a dreamless state of unconscious. This state induces healing and is a deep form of relaxation. Its use in hypnosis for pain relief is quite effective.

With modern technology, you can access each of these brain states by stimulating certain frequencies. This is brainwave entrainment.
When tones of different frequencies are presented to each ear individually, pulsations called Binaural Beats occur in the brain stem resulting in a stimulated brain state. Often these beats play behind a soft music or nature sounds and you listen to the music on stereo headphones and it will take you quickly to the brain state you want to achieve.
I have some of these tracks available on my website at www.tanyablack.com. You can download them as an mp3.
Baroque music such as Bach played at 60 beats to the minute has also shown similar benefits and an increase in retention.
I have an interest in advanced learning techniques and brain enhancement and it's applications in every facet of your life.
There are many tools for conscious control over your mental state. These are the ones I have found most effective. I have been using these techniques for many years and found they have helped me in many ways.
The other technique I use regularly is hypnosis. Hypnosis is a heightened state of awareness. It is an incredibly beneficial and effective way of stimulating and creating long-term change.
I used hypnosis for the birth of both of my children and practice it daily. I have my own compilations that I use with affirmations and guided meditation and have used it for increased memory retention and learning.

Other types of mental entrainment and clarity are achievable with various other methodologies. I'll list some of them here, but this list is just a basic overview and there are many other techniques available:

- *Meditation* – When you can learn to meditate and relax your whole body and let your thoughts float away, your body is renewed, your mind has a higher level of clarity and stress just drifts away.

- *Neuro Linguistic Programming* – Specific techniques I use are:

    Breaking State – If you find yourself getting angry or tense, do something completely off topic or distract yourself with something. It's is good tool for parents. If my children are crying because they hurt themselves, I will pretend I just saw a butterfly or something different and they quickly forget they were upset. It works just as effectively if you do it to yourself and distract yourself with something momentarily. Then look at the problem with fresh eyes.
    Disassociate – Separate yourself from the scenario. Pretend you are looking at the scenario from the outside with an objective view. Imagine you are in a cinema and the scene is playing out before you. Then think critically on how you could best approach the situation if you were one of the characters in that movie.
    Anchoring – place anchors and positive memory triggers all over your body. I once had someone use it on me for seduction. I won't tell you my trigger, but it was very sneaky.
    Once I figured it out, it did lift a veil of confusion but I kept the anchor. It made me happy so I fire it off myself now and then.

There's plenty of amazing NLP techniques you can use for seduction. They will make you irresistible and they work. If you are feeling a little innovative, have a look around the internet, try it and use your new powers for good.

'With great power comes great responsibility.' Stan Lee

- *Creative Expression and Art Therapy* – The exercise of creating, painting, expressing yourself and writing stimulates an Alpha frequency where you lose time.
  Specific exercises you can do are: contour drawing – focus on an object or person and let your pen try to capture every detail but don't lift your pen or look at your paper. It will look like a big scribble but it will put you straight into an alpha brain state.
  Another fun game to play to get into the Alpha mindset is 'Tangrams'. Tangrams are old Chinese puzzles using geometric shapes to copy a silhouette. They look deceptively simple but really expand your mind when you try to do them.

- *Kinesiology* – It uses movements to stimulate brain activity and learning.

- *The mental blackboard* – If you find yourself having a negative thought, picture it on a blackboard in your head. Picture yourself wiping it out and then write a positive thought on the blackboard instead and focus on it. It helps if you make it brighter and enhance the feelings that thought gives you. This one sounds a bit loopy, but is actually very effective.

- *The Bubble* – This is one I learned when I was doing the hypnosis for my childbirth. As many people are quite cynical when you tell them you will be using hypnosis for your pain relief during childbirth, you need to have a defence and a way of managing it.
  Picture a special place where you feel safe and completely relaxed. I visualised a beautiful place from the Gold Coast where I live called 'Natural Bridge' or 'Natural Arch'. It is heaven on earth. You will have your own place, whether it is a garden or a beach or somewhere that is all you own.

Focus on everything around you, the smells, the touch of your surrounds and the sounds and make it as real as possible.

Now imagine a large bubble around you and your special place. Nobody can get inside this bubble unless you want him or her there. You are perfectly safe within your bubble and your special place.

If someone is being aggressive, intimidating or patronising, all you can hear from within your bubble is a tap tap tap on the bubble, like a small bird pecking on a pane of glass. Meanwhile, you are blissfully and safely inside your special place.

Plant an anchor on your thumb. Anytime you squeeze the tip of your thumb, it activates the bubble and the more you use it the more effective it will be.

This one tool has saved me much heartache and helped me disassociate from many conflicting situations when I have not been in the right mindset to manage them.

Some day you will not need your bubble anymore and any conflict will pass right through you like a mist but until you feel strong enough to surrender and let go, the bubble is an effective mechanism for regaining clarity.

These are the main tools I use. There are countless others. Find what works for you.

A checklist you can take with you is to write out the following cues on a piece of card and carry it with you:

In Case of Emergency:

* Posture
* Smile
* Relax Jaw
* Focus on Breathing - 5 Deep Breaths counting backwards
* Glass of Water
* Break State
* Activate Bubble
* Disassociate
* Use your Positive Anchors

Figure 22.1 - Relaxation and Tension Relief Checklist

When you refer to it, doing all of these things will take no more than two minutes in total and will put you in a better mindset.

Spirituality - Many of us grow up with some form of religious background and we are all at least aware of the religions of the world. I choose to never criticise another person for their faith and it is important to keep an open mind when speaking with people who are passionate about their faith.

Everyone is entitled to their beliefs and opinions and even if they conflict with your own, it is your choice on how you will respond, communicate, and allow those opinions to affect you.

What people can accomplish with the power of faith and belief is inspiring. The act of meditating and quieting your mind as you listen to your deeper intuition is enough to give you the clarity you need to live your life to its highest potential.

Spirituality is the act of love in its purest energetic form. How you choose to access that love is a matter of personal preference. You may go to church. You might find your connection when you are out working in your garden.

You will know when you are connected and on that other level because you will feel a calm come over you. Your problems will dissolve and you will know and trust that everything will be as it is meant to be.

Some people access their spirituality by connecting with the earth using crystals. Others seek education on higher expression, psychic awareness, universal principles, and quantum physics. Some explore the laws of attraction. Some use their religion.

Others find a peace within themselves or have a love for their child or spouse.

It doesn't matter what form your spirituality takes. It's not what the faith and belief is that harbours the magic, it is the power, love, faith and belief itself that makes magic happen.

Try It!

Mind, Body and Spirit; the three elements of every person. Love who you are. Cherish yourself as you would a newborn baby. You are special. You are gifted. You are loved. Live and experience life. This is your Utopia. Make it worth the journey.

Do some further research on the processes that appeal to you and select a few that will fit in with your own preferences?

Explore your spirituality. Be open to listening to your intuition and your heart. Cry when you need to cry, and laugh when you feel joy. Feel and explore yourself and every emotion and depth you have within you.

Chapter Twenty-Three

Rome wasn't Built in a Day and the Universe took Seven

Taking each moment as it comes

Chapter Twenty-Three

"Don't just take what each day brings. Bring something to each day."

Tanya Black

This final story is a story about a woman who found something within herself that she always knew was there but never had the courage to act upon it.

She helped others achieve their best. She wouldn't take credit for her ideas and work for fear of ridicule. She feared being judged as up herself or a fraud.

One day she finally fell in a ravine so low that she could not fall any further. When she hit the floor of the ravine, she searched around for a friendly face and a helping hand.

She looked around expecting to find one of the faces she'd helped along the way, or hear a voice of encouragement from one of those whose ears she'd whispered empowering words to not so long ago. The ravine was silent and empty.

Naked on the floor of the ravine and stripped of her previous perceptions of contentment, she made a choice. She would scale the wall herself. Unaided, she would only look forward, never looking back.

She heard a voice within herself that told her she could do it if she focused her attention on her own dreams and goals and visions.

Step by step and inch by inch she moved closer. The sun started shining and she took each day at a time. Moment by moment, she focused on getting higher and higher and soon the sun was shining on her skin, and the sounds of birds singing tunes just for her brought her joy and fulfilment.

It does not matter where you are now, do not look down, and only look up at the view of possibility and potential and the infinite gifts awaiting you to receive them.

Don't eat the whole elephant. I imagine elephant probably tastes pretty rank anyway, but the phrase means to take life one bite at a time.

Try to take each day one day at a time. When you go to bed at night, put your thoughts to bed too. You can plan and write things in your diary before bed, but once you write them down, put them out of your mind. As you close you eyes to sleep, imagine your thoughts are mist. It might look like a thick fog at first if you have an active mind, let the mist drift away over a lake.

Another gizmo you could use is a 'thoughts bag'. Have a special little bag, a canvas bag or one that's pretty. At night time, pull the thoughts out of your head and put them in the bag. The physical act of doing this makes your brain shut off.

Leave the bag somewhere in your kitchen or lounge room. It's not to go anywhere near your bedroom or where you rest.

In the morning you can revisit those thoughts and take them out of the bag but once they are in there, they stay there for the night.

I also use this one when my children pick up mean words or colourful language. We put the mean words in the rubbish bag and throw them out. I always make this a fun exercise to shift their minds as well. I'll say things like 'Gross, that one had boogers on it,' and they will laugh and switch to a better frame of mind.

When you wake each morning, have some positive affirmations on your bedroom door, your bathroom mirror and your fridge. Read them. Be conscious of them and commit to applying them that day.

Create an anchor on your doorway. Anchors don't have to be specific to your body. I have an anchor on my doorway so that whenever I walk through it I feel confident and happy. I thought of every happy thought I could plant and a time when I felt confident and I planted it on my doorway. Whenever I walk out the door, that's how I feel.

A door is a great metaphor for new beginnings, so that anchor is very effective.

Plan each day, eat well, stay healthy and live each day on purpose.

Review your mind maps and plans periodically. Make the changes you need to make a step at a time until they become habits.

Measure your outcomes and take a moment each day to smile and appreciate that you are a beautiful person. You are in complete control of your outcomes.

Chapter Twenty-Three - Rome wasn't Built in a Day and the Universe took Seven

Reward yourself and allow for flexibility. If you allow yourself some periodic rewards, and take a moment to pat yourself on the back now and then, there is a stronger chance of you reaching your goals.

Take each day one step at a time. Decide on what you can do in that day and do it.

I hope I have given you something of value. I always welcome new friends and life experiences. I can be contacted via my website at www.tanyablack.com where I will be updating articles and adding tools and resources over time, or via my email at tanya@tanyablack.com

I have enjoyed writing this book. Thank you for reading it. I wish you well on your own journey and peace, good fortune and a fulfilling life.

To close I will repeat my closing paragraph from the beginning of the book:

Remember where you came from and appreciate how far you have come, but don't hold onto the past so tightly that you can't embrace the present and every opportunity it has to offer. Don't be blind to the riches that are yours now for the taking.

Be the Change.

Tanya Black

My Bucket List

When you are making changes and wanting to improve your life, don't be afraid to call on others for help.

Most people like to help each other out and networking can open doors and present opportunities that you may not have previously known.

One of the fun things I did when I set out on my new adventure was to write my bucket list – a list of various stuff I want to do in my lifetime.

I've achieved a couple of them already, but I'd like to test the theory of the six degrees of separation. If you know someone who knows someone who might want to be a part of the adventure, get in touch.

Behold - some of my Bucket List:

- Write and Publish a Book
- Appear on Oprah
- Get a Private Dance lesson from Justin Timberlake
- Learn Italian
- See the Sistine Chapel
- Learn to Surf
- Celebrate a New Years Eve in New York
- Take my kids to Disney
- When my book is printed - take the kids on a helicopter ride
- Play the role of Wonder Woman in a movie
- Win the Archibald Prize
- See the Incas
- Design and build a self sustaining strawbale house
- Get my pilot's license
- Learn the piano
- Learn the guitar
- Have a garden that looks like the Mt Tamborine Gardens

Resources

Recommended further reading:

Spirituality

Eckhart Toll - The Power of Now

Think and Grow Rich - Napoleon Hill

The Masterkey System - Charles F Haanel

The Science of Getting Rich - Wallace D. Wattles

Finance

Wealth Magic - Peter Spann

Multiple Streams of Income - Robert G Allen

Rich Dad Poor Dad - Robert Kyasaki

Supercharge your Trading with CFD's - Jeff Cartridge

Life Management/Business

The Business Coach - Brad Sugars

The E-myth Revisted - Michael E Gerber

The 80/20 Principle - Richard Koch

The Richest Man in Babylon - George S Clason

The Seven Habits of Highly Effective People - Stephen R Covey

The Ten Natural Laws of Successful Time and Life Management - Hyrum W Smith

Impact - Ken McArthur

The Irresistible Offer - Mark Joyner

Mastering Online Marketing - Mitch Meyerson

The 4 Hour Work Week - Tim Ferriss

www.ingramcontent.com/pod-product-compliance
Lightning Source LLC
Chambersburg PA
CBHW071708160426
43195CB00012B/1614